A D V A N C E   P R A I S E   F O R
Writing Dissent

"Robert Jensen has written a tremendous introduction to journalism for writer and citizen alike, a veritable how-to guide for anyone to enter the world of mainstream news and opinion making. Clear, well written, and to the point, there is nothing else like it. The book also includes examples of Jensen's own columns from the past few years, which are worth the price of the book by themselves. Readers will soon see why Jensen has emerged as one of the leading radical writers of our times."

Robert W. McChesney, Professor, University of Illinois;
Author of Rich Media, Poor Democracy

"Too often people with critical views give up on the mainstream press. *Writing Dissent* shows how it is possible to craft truly radical essays that can push and shove their way into publications that regular folks read. The breadth of contemporary politics dissected in Jensen's writing and his sensible firsthand accounts of how journalists work make this book invaluable."

Phyllis Bennis, Fellow of the Institute for Policy Studies;
Author of Calling the Shots: How Washington
Dominates Today's UN

"Robert Jensen's *Writing Dissent* is a real winner, combining earthy and practical advice on the writing of dissenting op-ed columns with an array of sample columns that are readable and enlightening in their own right."

Edward S. Herman, Professor Emeritus, University of
Pennsylvania; Co-Author of Manufacturing Consent

Writing Dissent

MEDIA & CULTURE

Sut Jhally & Justin Lewis
General Editors

Vol. 5

PETER LANG
New York • Washington, D.C./Baltimore • Bern
Frankfurt am Main • Berlin • Brussels • Vienna • Oxford

Robert Jensen

Writing Dissent

Taking Radical Ideas from the Margins to the Mainstream

PETER LANG
New York • Washington, D.C./Baltimore • Bern
Frankfurt am Main • Berlin • Brussels • Vienna • Oxford

Library of Congress Cataloging-in-Publication Data

Jensen, Robert.
Writing dissent: taking radical ideas
from the margins to the mainstream / Robert Jensen.
p. cm. — (Media and culture; vol. 5)
Includes bibliographical references and index.
1. Journalism—Political aspects. 2. Radicalism in mass media.
I. Title. II. Media & culture (New York, N.Y.); vol. 5.
PN4751 .K46   302.23—dc21   2001029252
ISBN 0-8204-5651-9
ISSN 1098-4208

Die Deutsche Bibliothek-CIP-Einheitsaufnahme

Jensen, Robert:
Writing dissent: taking radical ideas
from the margins to the mainstream / Robert Jensen.
–New York; Washington, D.C./Baltimore; Bern;
Frankfurt am Main; Berlin; Brussels; Vienna; Oxford: Lang.
(Media & culture; Vol. 5)
ISBN 0-8204-5651-9

Cover design by Joni Holst

The paper in this book meets the guidelines for permanence and durability
of the Committee on Production Guidelines for Book Longevity
of the Council of Library Resources.

© 2001, 2003, 2004, 2005 Peter Lang Publishing, Inc., New York
275 Seventh Avenue, 28th Floor, New York, NY 10001
www.peterlangusa.com

Printed in the United States of America

To the memory of Sally Koplin and the struggle for a better world.

Table of Contents

Acknowledgments

The material in this book is the product of both my professional training as a journalist inside this society's mainstream institutions and my political education outside those institutions. As a journalist, I worked with—and learned from—many decent and talented people. Since leaving the mainstream of the profession, I have become quite critical of the structures and practices of contemporary journalism, but I retain affection for the craft and the people. One of those journalists, Charles Spencer, has remained a valued friend and informal editor. His sense of humor has often injected much-needed levity into long days at the keyboard, and his commitment to his own work constantly reminds me of what it means to be a writer.

My political education began with my work in the feminist antipornography and antiviolence movement in Minneapolis, where I benefited from the experience and wisdom of Sally Koplin, Jeanne Barkey, Donna McNamara, and Jim Koplin. This book is dedicated to the memory of Sally, and in a larger sense to everyone who worked with her and was touched by her kindness as well as her fierce and unbending commitment to justice.

That political education moved forward through work with, and the friendship of, the members of the Nowar Collective in Austin, Texas: Rahul Mahajan, Romi Mahajan, and Zeynep. I will be forever grateful to them not just for what they taught me about politics and the world, but also for the way in which they taught me. For three years we have argued and laughed our way through political and personal issues in a fashion that has reshaped the way I understand the world and try to live in it.

Two faculty colleagues at the University of Texas, Kamala Visweswaran and Miguel Ferguson, have been good friends and steady allies, making it much easier to be politically active on a conservative campus.

Finally, special thanks to Lane Browning, who read and reacted to many of the essays in this book as they were being formulated and written, but whose influence on this book goes beyond simple editing. The years in which I was writing the material in this book were ones of great change for me—political, professional, and personal—and I can see Lane's influences throughout the pages of this book.

Introduction

Mainstreaming Dissent

For the past few years I have spent a good chunk of my writing time on opinion and analysis articles for mainstream daily newspapers. Whatever the subject—foreign policy, war, economics, race, sexual harassment—my goal has been to put together pieces offering unvarnished analysis that may seem too radical for such mainstream channels yet that can find its way into one of those mainstream channels. When I publish pieces that identify the United States as a terrorist nation or condemn the values inherent in capitalism, the response I often get from friends, political colleagues, and readers is: "That was really radical. How did you manage to get that into the paper?" This book is an attempt to answer that question and help others get their radical analysis into the mainstream.

People who write lots of newspaper columns often pause every couple of years, gather up the columns, and publish them as a book, on the assumption that what was written for quick consumption at a particular moment in time will be of enduring interest. I do not make that assumption, and I hope to do something a bit different here. I want first to show readers that anyone can write and get published in the mainstream. Although I trade on my position as a former journalist and university professor, which sometimes helps on the credibility front, I'm not a well-known person who can get published solely on name recognition. With a couple of exceptions, I do not write pieces that are guaranteed space; most of what I write is "on spec," with no promise that any editor would pick it up. If I can do it, so can anyone else.

Once readers see that it is possible to write, I want to offer some strategies for getting published. There are lots of guides to working with the news media that provide basic tips for writing op/eds and dealing with editors. In this book, I want to go beyond those basics by explaining how specific columns came together in my computer, and then came to be in the newspaper. My hope is that readers will leave the book with confidence about their own abilities. Journalists and writers often like to pretend that what

they do requires some special ability or natural gift. I often hear
people comment, "Oh, I could never write a piece like that," or "I
just don't know how to write." There is nothing magical about
journalistic writing. There is room for creativity but within a
clearly defined format; it is a craft that can be learned by almost
everyone who wants to commit the time and energy. I know,
because that is what I did. I'm not a particularly creative writer.
I've never written a poem (at least not one I would show to anyone else), short story, or novel. I have no natural gifts. I learned a
craft. So can anyone.

Still, a key question remains: "Is writing for the mainstream
media worth the time and effort?" Left/progressive/radical people
should always ask that question. Are there other ways to use one's
time that are potentially more productive than trying to shoehorn
700 words into the local daily paper?

There can be no one answer to that question for all people in
all situations; contingencies, political and personal, may argue for
different choices in different times and places. But in general, it
makes sense to think of media strategy for radicals as having three
basic components: production of, and support for, alternative
media; criticism of mainstream media, both in public and directly
to journalists; and use of the mainstream media when possible.
(This framework is borrowed from Charlotte Ryan; see her book
Prime Time Activism.)

The first component of that strategy is obvious. Alternative
media are crucial in providing the kind of in-depth information
and analysis that radical political projects and social movements
need. We cannot rely on corporate-owned, commercial media to
do that for us. Equally important is the task of monitoring and
critiquing the news and opinions in the mainstream media, both
to hold journalists accountable and to influence their story selection and reporting, and to let the public know (through letters to
the editor, media monitor publications, and nonmediated public
education) what they are, and are not, getting in their daily news
fare.

For similar reasons, we should be trying to use the mainstream
media, both by getting journalists to cover our stories (and cover
them honestly and accurately) as well as by getting our own
writing and reporting into those channels when possible. There

are many different strategies and tactics in this battle, perhaps the most obvious of which is the newspaper op/ed. Although the op/ed pages are filled mostly with syndicated columnists and staff writers, most newspapers on occasion give space to work submitted from readers, activists, and independent journalists.

As long as the majority of Americans get the majority of their information from these conventional mass media sources, it will be important for radicals to exploit the opportunities that exist to use these media to try to expand our movements and reach new people. My own experience makes it clear that such op/eds have an effect, not just on those who already agree with me but on people who are uncertain about an issue. I have received hundreds of calls, letters, and emails about my pieces that run in newspapers and then often float around the Internet via discussion lists and Web sites.

This experience doesn't definitively answer the question of whether it is a better use of my time to research, write and work at getting an op/ed published, as opposed to building alternative media or organizing a letter-writing campaign or any number of other activities. Whatever answer I arrive at will be a mixture of hunches; there is no way to conduct a survey to see what the effect of any single political activity might be. In the final analysis, it is a product not just of political assessment but individual talents and temperaments. In the final chapter, I'll return to the question. For now, let's turn to politics.

PART I
GETTING READY TO WRITE

Chapter 1

What Makes Radical Analysis Radical?

The strategies I will talk about in the rest of the book can be applied in some fashion to the task of getting any political viewpoint into the newspaper. But my focus is on how to get radical ideas into the mainstream, which should raise the question, "What do you mean by radical?"

One standard response to that question is to remind people of the origins of the word—radical, from the Latin *radicalis*, meaning "root." Radical analysis goes to the root of an issue or problem. Typically that means that while challenging the specific manifestations of a problem, radicals also analyze the ideological and institutional components as well as challenge the unstated assumptions and conventional wisdom that obscure the deeper roots. Often it means realizing that what is taken as an aberration or deviation from a system is actually the predictable and/or intended result of a system.

For example, on almost any economic issue, mainstream liberals and conservatives can be found fighting about the ins and outs of a particular policy. For example, should the capital gains tax be lowered or raised? Those who stay within the conventional analysis will not address basic questions of the justice of the whole system. What goes unasked is a more central question: Why should we accept a system in which some individuals are allowed to accumulate large fortunes while others work much harder but have no material security? Radical critics of capitalism would not lose sight of the root cause of the problem: the fundamental structures and values of capitalism and the contemporary corporate system.

Or, take the issue of rape. No reasonable person endorses rape, but many people see it simply as the bad behavior of individuals to be addressed through the criminal justice system or psychological intervention. From a radical feminist perspective, the problem is not primarily pathological individuals (though they do exist and do rape) but the patriarchal values and institutions that lead allegedly "normal" men to rape and allow a society to minimize the problem. Rape, in this sense, is normal—the expression of male-supremacist values that make domination and control sexy. Core definitions of gender, sex, and power have to be addressed for wide-reaching progress to be possible.

This focus of analysis is particularly relevant to the question of publishing op/eds because, in general, the more radical the analysis is perceived to be, the less likely it will be published. It should be no surprise that editors who mostly have lived and worked within conventional political frameworks are not predisposed to seek out challenges to the fundamental structures of society (more on that in the next chapter). This is not a reason to water down one's analysis, but it makes it important to be clear about what one's underlying critique is, so that thoughtful decisions can be made about when to push closer to the radical edge and when to hold back.

In our political lives, most of us on a daily basis make compromises to achieve short-term political goals, and similar decisions have to be made in op/ed writing. Radical union activists who believe in the dismantling of capitalism often work for relatively small gains for workers within a capitalist system, but they don't buy into propaganda about management-worker partnerships that can so easily co-opt radical organizing. Radical feminists who believe that the institutions of government are patriarchal to the core will sometimes work within those institutions to pass laws that expand women's rights, but they don't believe that the existing legal system can guarantee sexual freedom and justice for all. As we work on various projects we often knowingly put aside some of the more radical demands, but that does not mean we give up a radical analysis. It remains crucial that we continue to talk about the underlying critique—not to make sure we stay loyal to some abstract theory for the sake of ideological purity, but because a systematic analysis is necessary to guide us as we make decisions about those short-term strategic compromises.

Beyond a few simple observations about the general targets of radical analysis, there is little one can say about what it means to be radical that would gather endorsement from all people who consider themselves radical, and that's perhaps as it should be. There are many different approaches to social issues that are radical, some of which are in conflict. My goal in this chapter is to sketch the political, social, and economic analysis that underlies the op/eds you will read in the rest of the book.

My own political philosophy is a synthesis of radical feminism, critical race theory, nonsectarian/anarchist-socialist anticapitalism, and neo-Luddite approaches to technology and ecology. As one would expect, such a constellation of ideas does not meet with universal agreement in left/progressive circles. Rather than try to define the terms "left" and "progressive," I will throughout the book stick with the concept of radical critique, realizing that not all critique that is radical is left-wing in traditional terms. I consider my own politics to be radical and left, but I'm not terribly concerned about defining the latter at this moment in history. Rather, I will try to explain how these different strands of thought fit together to create my sense of politics.

There is a contentious argument among left/progressives about the role of identity-based movements in the broad struggle for justice. Put simply, some more traditional leftists contend that a focus on issues of race, gender, and sexual orientation has splintered the progressive world and derailed attention from core questions of economic inequality. Perhaps because my own introduction to radical politics came through feminism, and the most radical part of the feminist movement, I have never felt that identity politics and anticapitalist politics were in conflict. Of course there are often strategic decisions about tactics and use of resources that are difficult to make because of conflicting needs and aims, but the painful divide that has opened has always seemed unnecessary to me. Rather than analyze where it came from and who is to blame, I want to tell my own story in brief.

While in graduate school, I got involved (first in scholarly work and then through activism) in the antipornography and antiviolence movement. My work on the radical feminist analysis of sexuality and male dominance was the first time I studied in-depth a radical analysis, and it not only educated me about those subjects but gave me a framework for analysis that I could use elsewhere. The key insight of that analysis for me was in seeing how what I had previously seen as "normal" sexuality was based on a dynamic of domination and submission, and that I had internalized that dynamic so thoroughly that it was invisible to me. It simply was the way things were (see, for example, the work of Andrea Dworkin and Catharine MacKinnon).

When I look at contemporary political issues in the United States, I see that same process playing out in every realm of power. There exist in the world many relationships of unequal power, in which one person or group has the ability to control another person or group. The people in the dominant position get something they want from that imbalance of power, and most of them either actively work to shore up their dominance or passively aid in the maintenance of the system by their refusal to challenge the inequities. Part of both strategies by the powerful is to argue that the imbalance is not the product of their choices, or of coercion or violence, but is in fact a natural phenomenon, an inevitable result of human nature. Often people in the subordinated group internalize the ideological claim and accept their status. In this manner, a system of power and control that is the product of social relations becomes invisible—just the way things are in the world.

The results are predictable. Men are taken to be dominant over women because men are stronger or smarter or more aggressive by nature, and women are happier in separate spheres where more feminine virtues can blossom. Whites are seen as dominant over nonwhites because of intellectual or cultural superiority that is an inevitable product of biology or history, or both. Heterosexual sex is considered natural because, after all, it can produce children; hence gays and lesbians are unnatural. The wealthy are believed to have more power than the poor because the wealthy have simply maximized their talents and capacity for work in a system that provides everyone equal opportunity to do that. The United States, with its distinctive history and mission, claims it is simply taking its natural role as leader in the international arena, shouldering the moral burden for a world that is dangerously chaotic.

From this view, the dynamic of domination and subordination is not a social problem to be addressed but a natural fact to be accepted. People of good faith who are in the dominant position can, and some might say should, do their best to protect the subordinated from the more harsh effects of these realities. But it would be folly to believe that eliminating the hierarchy is possible, or even desirable, according to those who promote, defend, and rationalize inequality.

This is the central logic of all systems of oppression. The logic plays out differently in different times and places, but understanding the pattern should help to connect all the liberatory movements in the contemporary world. Just as men are not naturally dominant over women, whites are not naturally dominant over nonwhites, heterosexuals are not naturally dominant over lesbians and gays, the wealthy are not naturally dominant over the poor, and Americans are not naturally dominant over the rest of the world. All these relationships of power are the product not of human nature but of social relations. They are imposed through violence or the threat of violence, and maintained through ideological control and ongoing force of varying intensity.

This obviously is not an attempt to construct an elaborate theory of liberatory politics; such attempts at universal theory (if we are to use the term "theory" in a meaningful way) in the social and political realm are bound to fail. Instead, I offer these simple statements as reminders that genuinely liberatory politics in real coalitions, across categories and issues, is possible, in part because the underlying dynamics of oppression are understandable across categories and issues. It is not to say that misogyny is exactly like racism, which is exactly like heterosexism, which is exactly like economic exploitation, which is exactly like contemporary imperialism. It is to say, however, that understanding one can lead to a broader understanding of them all. The factionalism that identity politics sometimes creates is not an inevitable outcome of attention to identity issues, and we do not have to bury those identity questions for the sake of some mythical coherent progressive movement. In fact, a genuinely progressive movement is impossible without some form of identity politics.

Analysis that can lead to meaningful action requires us to see patterns in how power is exercised; without such pattern perception, we would never know how or where to challenge the power. As we do that, of course, we have to see how patterns are not the whole story. As in much of life, in politics we have to struggle with balancing the need to create categories and use them in analysis, with the need to honor the particularity and difference that confound categories. The theory that guides us has to not only remain grounded in the world, but it has to acknowledge its limitations. As smart as humans can be, it is our ignorance that we should be most conscious of. We do not, as a species, have the intellectual capacity to make sense of everything. We must be able at the same time to hold onto the courage of our convictions while acknowledging the always evolving nature of our understanding and analysis.

My own political life illustrates these points. From my initial work on radical feminist projects, I became increasingly interested in questions of sexual orientation (see, for example, Marilyn Frye and Sarah Hoagland) and race (see, for example, W.E.B. DuBois and Ward Churchill). From those identity questions, I expanded my study and interests to economic structures, which led to a more active interest in foreign policy and U.S. actions abroad (see, for example, William Blum and Noam Chomsky). Through it all, I have remained connected to questions of sustainability. My writing and political activism have, at one point or another, dealt with all these issues. Identity politics, for me, did not derail a holistic analysis; it was the motivation for and means to that analysis. Sometimes I am critical of certain people or positions within identity politics (for example, I have argued with many white, middle-class gay men about their failure to critique capitalism and to take race and gender issues seriously), but that does not mean that identity politics must lead to a narrowing of anyone's analysis of social justice.

I continue to work on projects and in movements that touch on all these concerns, and often one issue encompasses multiple concerns. One cannot talk about foreign policy, for example, without explicitly addressing economic issues and racism. Foreign policy is driven by the interests of corporate capitalism, and U.S. interventions and brutalities abroad are often more palatable to the public because they tap into the unspoken assumptions about the superiority of white European culture. Those kinds of connections are integral to understanding systems and fashioning responses.

I have left for the end a discussion of a neo-Luddite view of technology and ecology that focuses on sustainability, in part because I find it is the most contentious aspect of my political philosophy in many radical circles. Neo-Luddites take the name from the early nineteenth-century Luddite movement in England, where textile workers resisted the introduction of new machines and the factory system of production. Often portrayed as ignorant opponents of progress (in most circles today, "Luddite" is an insult, synonymous with a kind of unthinking resistance to change), the original Luddites were not against all machines, only those "hurtful to Commonality," machines used in systems that would destroy communities (see Kirkpatrick Sale).

Likewise, contemporary neo-Luddites are often tagged as being antitechnology, which is a silly label. Humans have always used, and will continue to use, technologies of varying kinds; the crucial questions concern the implications of the advanced technologies our society creates and uses. There is no one statement of a neo-Luddite philosophy, but in general those of us who identify with the concept, like the original Luddites, reject technologies that tend to be destructive to human lives and communities and, more broadly, reject the notion that social progress is tied to technological development.

Another key notion is that technologies are always political and never neutral; they reflect the interests of those who designed them. That doesn't mean that a technology created for war cannot be used for anything else (the Internet, with its origins in the U.S. Department of Defense, is the most obvious recent example). Rather, it is to argue simply that technologies created for use in an increasing impersonal mass society likely will in some ways help perpetuate such a society (again, the Internet is a good example). The solutions to human problems lie in human relationships, not technologies, and the solution to problems created by technologies rarely is more technology; unintended consequences continue the cycle of problem creation and "solution" without addressing the underlying questions of the scale and scope of humans' capacity to run the world with such unreflective hubris.

One practical application of these ideas can be seen in the sustainable agriculture movement, which focuses on how "modern" agriculture—the imposition of "scientific" techniques, the use of massive amounts of chemicals and petroleum, and the influence of corporate interests—devastates both rural communities and the natural world. Technologies designed to increase food production have costs that threaten our long-term survival (see Wendell Berry and Wes Jackson).

The framework of domination and subordination is helpful here. Technological societies work on a logic of domination of nature and the nonhuman world, captured in Rene Descartes' comment in his *Discourse on Method* that people could begin to understand the physical world in order to "render ourselves the masters and possessors of nature." Unlike the other oppressive relationships, this entails not the creation of hierarchies among people, but the assertion of a basic hierarchy in which the interests of humans trump the interests of all other living things. The result is a world out of balance in which the possibility of sustained life, human and nonhuman, is called into question. Pick virtually any measure of sustainability—toxic waste accumulation, soil erosion, resource depletion, global warming—and it is clear that we have so accelerated the rate of attack on, and neglect of, the nonhuman world that talk of the end of life as we know it is no longer the province solely of doomsayers with apocalyptic visions (for a review of where we stand, see Ed Ayres).

To bring these various ideas together, I would offer a truism that we should make central in our politics: Unsustainable systems cannot be sustained indefinitely. Systems that do not take into account the costs as well as the benefits of certain activities will eventually grind to a halt and likely will do extreme damage in the meantime. A slightly more contentious statement is: Any system that is premised on a dynamic of domination and subordination is unsustainable. There is no way to prove the second claim; it is based on my experience and observation. But in broad terms it echoes analyses emerging in other liberatory ideologies and movements, such as some strands of ecofeminism and indigenous rebellions such as the Zapatistas in Chiapas.

At the core of all these ideas for me is a basic resistance to the naturalizing of power inequities. Any system that suggests domination is obviously appropriate and natural is to be rejected; the imposition of power and authority by a person or group on another person or group must always be justified. As Noam Chomsky has put it:

"Any structure of hierarchy and authority carries a heavy burden of justification, whether it involves personal relations or a larger social order. If it cannot bear the burden...then it is illegitimate and should be dismantled. When honestly posed and squarely faced, that challenge can rarely be sustained" (Chomsky 1996, p. 73).

To make progress on these issues, it is important to talk not only about politics but about morality. Discussion of values and morals has of late been territory occupied almost exclusively by the right-wing, especially the fundamentalist Christian right. I believe radical movements must not be afraid to acknowledge the central questions underneath all these issues: What does it mean to be a human being? What is human nature? What are people for? These questions are, of course, in some sense unanswerable. At best we can make tentative claims based on imperfect information and then continue to challenge ourselves and our ideas. I will end this chapter with a few observations that are quite simple but important to articulate and constantly engage.

Unless one reverts to an unquestioning belief in a divine text or puts an irrational faith in the ability of the social sciences to answer what, in the end, are unanswerable questions, we are never going to have anything beyond partial clues to the question of what is human nature. The quest for certainty in this realm is doomed from the start. But what we can observe is that humans engage in a range of behaviors, and that different social structures offer different rewards and punishments that tend to channel members of the society toward certain behaviors and away from others. There are patterns, but great variation within the patterns. Our behavior is always the product of who we are as determined by our common human nature rooted in our biology (which we know very little about), who we are as determined by our individual natures (which we also don't know much about), who the society in which we live wants and allows us to be (which is complex, often with conflicting demands), and who we will ourselves to be (through agency that is both fostered and limited by those social structures). Little beyond the speculative can be said about the proportions of the mix, and it seems to me to be sensible to concentrate on what we have some control over—social structures and individual actions.

Given this wide range of behaviors one sees in the world, it seems clear that human nature gives us: the capacity for creativity that can be expressed in diverse fashions; an instinct for pursuing self-interest that is balanced with compassion, solidarity, and mutual respect; a yearning for freedom that is complicated by, but not necessarily smothered by, the unavoidable constraints that come with social life; and a sense of our place in a human world wider than our own specific places. I also believe we have the capacity to understand, in ecological terms, our place within a natural system and the limits that system imposes on us.

I have no proof, in traditional terms, for these claims, though they are based on real-world observation and experience. Still, while not wholly subjective, these choices also are based largely on faith, not in a force outside of people but in people. Rather than assert this view of human nature as an unassailable claim, I offer it more as a starting point for discussion, which strikes me as the right way to approach questions that, in the end, we cannot answer definitively or even with very much confidence. Part of being human, I believe, is going forward knowing that, however ignorant we are, we must choose, and that our choices matter.

Chapter 2

Understanding Journalism
and Journalists

It is not terribly difficult to understand contemporary U.S. journalism and journalists. As is often the case, people standing outside a profession can, in some ways, critique the field better than those folks working in it. When I was a working journalist for mainstream newspapers, I knew how to do my job but I often didn't know the social function of the job I was doing. By that I mean that while inside the newsroom, I couldn't see some of the structural and ideological constraints under which I worked. Some journalists can see through these while right in the middle of them; most can't, and I wasn't able to either. Although I was fairly critical of the hierarchy and bureaucracy of the newsroom, I accepted most of the professional norms of journalism, and hence I didn't have the clearest view of what I was doing.

Since leaving journalism for academic life, I have spent considerable time and energy trying to understand better journalists and journalism. In this chapter I want to explain how newsrooms are organized, describe how journalists see their own work, and suggest effective ways for activists to approach journalists.

I want to be clear that the critique I offer here comes from affection: I like journalists. Some of my best friends are, and have been, journalists. I was a journalist. In some ways, I still am. I believe in the power of journalism as it has been practiced by the likes of Tom Paine, Frederick Douglass, Ida B. Wells, W.E.B. DuBois, George Seldes, and I.F. Stone. In my own life I have met the contemporary counterparts of those famous historical names, journalists such as Gary Webb, Allan Nairn, and P. Sainath, folks who inspire me.

But I also am a critic of my craft, often a harsh one, because it is so clear that most journalism rarely measures up to the ideal of holding the powerful accountable. Sometimes, when I judge journalists to be impediments to real understanding of issues and barriers to social justice, I find myself thinking that I hate journalists. But the hatred is not for the people in mainstream news-rooms; it is for the structures that make it difficult for decent people to do good work in those newsrooms.

I have worked at everything from a small weekly newspaper with a few thousand subscribers to a metropolitan daily. I have worked in rural areas, the suburbs, and cities. I have been a re-porter, photographer, and copy editor. I have worked for an after-noon paper, which meant getting up at 4 a.m., and for a morning paper that kept me at work until after midnight. I have worked for first-rate editors with great instincts and integrity, and I have worked for third-rate editors with no news judgment who were company lackies. I was the kind of journalist management gener-ally likes—not flashy but dependable. Folks like me populate newsrooms around the country and do the not terribly glamorous work of covering city council meetings, shuffling through police reports, writing headlines, and making sure everything fits on the page. We fill a newspaper efficiently. We accept often embarrass-ingly low wages (unless we work at a unionized publication), in part because we have internalized the belief that journalists are the front-line troops defending democracy.

Since leaving the industry, I have continued to work and talk with journalists, read the trade press, and keep up on changes in the industry. I also have read a lot of scholarly research on jour-nalism (some of which is actually worth reading). So, I believe I am in a good position to talk about what journalists do and how they do it, and I think my advice for dealing with journalists is trustworthy.

(I'll use the term "journalists" throughout, but I am really talk-ing about reporters and editors who work at commercial newspa-pers and broadcast outlets—the kind of papers and stations that are out to make a profit and usually are owned by corporations, whether it be a small family company or a huge media conglom-erate. There are, of course, lots of other kinds of journalists in the world, but I'm focusing on those who work for the institutions that provide the majority of Americans with their news.)

One thing to remember: Journalists are people, too. By that I mean that they have the same needs as anyone else. Although they pride themselves on being cranky and make it clear they don't expect to be loved for what they do, it is my experience that the vast majority of journalists want to do their jobs competently and ethically and be appreciated for it. They don't enjoy being criticized or told they are ignorant. Most will 'fess up to a mistake, but they would prefer not to have their noses rubbed in it.

Another thing: With the exception of those journalists at the highest levels who have been allowed to specialize, most reporters and editors are generalists. They know a little bit about a lot of things so that they can drop into any story and do a competent job. They rarely bring expertise from outside journalism to their jobs.

Those two facts are crucial to understand when working with mainstream journalists. Serious activists who have spent time and energy learning an issue are almost always better informed than the journalists with whom they are dealing. Yet journalists rarely can acknowledge that, no matter how obvious it is; to do so would put them in a position of professional weakness. This means that no matter how angry activists might get at coverage that is inaccurate or distorted, they have to learn to repress the anger and deal with journalists on the journalists' terms. In most cases, the journalists will be happy for the help, as long as the help doesn't require capitulation on their part.

I offer this advice knowing I haven't always put it into practice. In a few situations I have been so angry or annoyed at an editor that I have argued openly and, in one case, committed the cardinal sin in dealing with journalists: I made the editor feel stupid by pointing out what he didn't know. He never directly acknowledged that, but it was painfully obvious from the conversation, and I don't think he ever forgave me for it. That mistake had consequences, not just for my ability to get op/eds in that paper, but for all the political movements and groups that I'm associated with in that editor's eyes.

The other surefire way to alienate journalists is to accuse them of bias or unfairness. In some sense, that accusation often is accurate, but it rarely is effective in nudging journalists to broaden their view or change their practices. In order to think through strategies for engaging journalists, it's important to think through the question of bias—what is meant by the term, as well as the limits of and alternatives to using that framework for critique.

Journalists for commercial media run on the craft norms of objectivity, neutrality, and balance. In theory, this means that journalists should not go into reporting a story with preconceived notions or intentions to favor any particular side of a story and that they should always be looking to present the issues from the point of view of all those affected by a story. Some aspects of those ideals are noble, but some are incoherent. And in practice, the norms and routines of journalists can make it more difficult to get at an accurate assessment of a situation. Many journalists have begun to acknowledge this, and it is common in the industry for people to say they aren't striving for objectivity, which is impossible, but for fairness. The problem is that the underlying norms and routines don't change, which means that changing the labels is meaningless.

So how should we think about professional norms? What should journalists strive for?

Let's start by looking at the basic problem with the concept of bias. There is a long, ongoing debate in philosophy and other disciplines about the status of facts and truth claims. An in-depth review of that debate is not necessary here. It is enough to point out that to say an account of the world is biased is to presume that there is some account possible that is not biased, that there is a rock-solid truth about the world that humans can observe, assess, and describe. Many statements about the world are so widely agreed upon as to be, for all practical purposes, the truth about the world (such as, "I am typing on a laptop computer right now" or "George Washington was the first president of the United States"). But while those claims—what I call the "brute facts" about the world—sometimes are subject to dispute, they are not typically what people argue about. What we generally debate is the selection and interpretation of those brute facts—we argue about what the facts of the matter mean and how those facts relate to bigger truths.

On matters of interpretation, it is difficult to make absolute claims about truth. We can marshal evidence and reasoning to support our interpretations, but there are always counterarguments and conflicting interpretations. In this sense, we all are biased. The question isn't who is and who isn't biased, but what is the quality of one's evidence and reasoning (and, often, who gets to set the rules for evaluating the evidence and reasoning). That means one of the key questions is about how open the discussion is to the widest possible range of arguments, and how responsive participants are to challenges. In mainstream journalism, the problem often is that the discussion takes place within a narrow spectrum, and powerful people typically are not forced to defend their claims against challenges.

It is important to talk in more detail about what shapes a reporter's interpretations. When most people make claims that journalists are biased, they mean that individuals who make news decisions favor one side of an argument over others. This is the point journalists are most willing to concede, because not to concede it is nonsensical. Obviously, individuals are the product of a variety of experiences and personal beliefs that influence how they see the world and, hence, how they cover the world. Unless journalists work hard not to know things, they are no different than other people—they will have made judgments about issues. My own experience is that because they have more access to information than average folks and are trained to make quick judgments, journalists have quite clear opinions about most everything. But that level of influence on news content—the biases of individual journalists—is the least serious. More important, but less visible, are the institutional and ideological influences.

Here, the propaganda model of Edward Herman and Noam Chomsky (see their book *Manufacturing Consent*, Herman's *The Myth of the Liberal Media*, and Chomsky's *Necessary Illusions*) is enlightening. By highlighting the political economy of mass media, Herman and Chomsky point out that how an institution is organized and funded, and the societal and political context in which it operates, are important in shaping the news. Their metaphor of news filters (size, concentration, and profit orientation of mass media; advertising as a primary revenue source; reliance on official sources of news; "flak" from wealthy and powerful segments of society as a means of disciplining the media; and anticommunism and free-market ideology as a national religion and control mechanism) helps us understand, in broad terms, how journalists work. More micro-level ethnographic and participant-observation studies (such as Gaye Tuchman's *Making News*) simply chart how the macro-level forces operate on a day-to-day basis.

So, talking about how "biases" affect news content has to go beyond the level of the individual journalist to look at institutional factors. The shape of news is very much a product of the for-profit nature of advertising-driven news in hierarchically organized corporations. Likewise, at the ideological level, journalists are very much affected by the society's taken-for-granted assumptions about the world: that capitalism and democracy are compatible, that free markets exist and produce a fair distribution of goods and services, that the United States conducts itself in a generally benevolent fashion in the world. These core ideas, which should be the subject of ongoing debate, are in fact mostly off the table for debate.

The response by journalists to these critiques is that professional norms and practices provide the corrective for both individual and institutional biases. The so-called firewall that separates the newsroom from the advertising department of a newspaper is said to insulate working reporters and editors from the economic forces that might want to shape the news. Meanwhile, journalists will explain that inside the newsroom they make decisions about selecting, reporting, and writing the news based on neutral professional criteria of newsworthiness, not ideology. There is some truth to these arguments; some of the obvious intrusions of the powerful into news content can be fended off by invoking those norms, and most journalists make a serious effort to make sure their personal viewpoints do not directly shape the news they write and edit. But that explanation doesn't account for the larger forces that shape the news. A few examples should suffice.

In the mainstream media, crime news is reported almost exclusively from the point of view of police and other officials in the criminal justice system. Why? Mostly because police reports and court records provide a low-cost source of news and afford wide protection from libel lawsuits. Add to that the tendency of journalists, most of whom are white and middle-class, to identify more with the police and prosecutors than with folks charged with crimes, and the result is predictable.

Or take most coverage of business. Though the press is often accused of being antibusiness, coverage of economics and the business world at mainstream newspapers and broadcast outlets takes as a given that corporate capitalism is a just and reasonable system. Even when running stories critical of individuals or businesses, those assumptions are not challenged, which produces news that is overwhelmingly probusiness. (See the essay on the press and business at the end of this chapter.)

Finally, as Herman and Chomsky exhaustively document in their book, coverage of U.S. foreign policy and military operations is almost without exception in line with government policy. Though sometimes willing to critique strategy and tactics, mainstream journalists almost never cast a critical eye on assumptions about the right of the United States to intervene militarily abroad and rarely ask tough questions about support for dictators who happen to serve the interests of U.S. policymakers.

From there, let's go back to the concepts of objectivity, neutrality, and balance, and assess their value in understanding news.

If objectivity means agreement not to make up facts that one knows not to be true, then I can think of no one who is against objectivity. If it means a good-faith attempt to acknowledge one's predispositions and assumptions when reporting a story, then again we could get widespread agreement on its value. The problem is that objectivity in journalism really means a set of practices that privilege official sources who reflect the powerful in society and fail to challenge the underlying assumptions of society. In that sense, I'm against objectivity.

Neutrality is even more problematic. First, it is clear that neutrality is selectively applied. No one would want journalists who are neutral on, say, the routine use of torture on children who misbehave in school, or on whether or not the Holocaust was morally wrong. I assume we all would want journalists who are outraged about these cruelties and would channel that outrage into vigorous reporting. Those examples cause us little concern, for there is wide agreement. But when issues get stickier— whether or not U.S. forces in Yugoslavia engaged in war crimes, for example—mainstream journalists not only are not allowed to be neutral but must get in step with the powerful in society; the working assumption was that the United States could not be guilty of war crimes. Claiming to be neutral, then, is simply a cover for adherence to the status quo and the opinions of the powerful.

Balance is just as troublesome. Take a story in which there are conflicting accounts of an issue. If a reporter had good reason to believe that one account was in fact less compelling, should the story be balanced to give each side roughly equal space? Should the reporter treat all claims in balanced fashion, even if one of the claims clearly can't be supported by the evidence? (See the op/ed on objectivity at the end of this chapter.)

Or take election coverage, in which most folks would agree that coverage of the viable candidates should be balanced. But which candidates count as viable? What is the gauge of viability? Standing in polls? But if one candidate is routinely boxed out of mass media coverage, how can she/he be expected to make a dent in the polls? It is easy to argue that writing more about minor-party and independent candidates (who generally lack the money of Republicans and Democrats to push themselves on the public) is necessary to provide the balance needed for an honest electoral system. From this view, balanced reporting about the major candidates based on professional norms does a disservice to readers.

Casting aside terms such as these and replacing them with "fairness" as a standard changes nothing, for the same issues arise. In short, the professional norms and practices do not guarantee that news is free from taint and bias but instead impoverish news coverage and yoke it to the status quo.

However powerful that kind of critique, most journalists don't buy it, which is not surprising. You would find it difficult to work within a system if you believed the system prevented you from doing your job in an honest and ethical fashion. It is also important to acknowledge that newsrooms are not monolithic, that in any system of social control there are opportunities to move outside the system's expectations. Good journalists understand the contradictions of the system and use them to their advantage. But rarely are mainstream journalists willing to accept a left/progressive critique of how power operates in a newsroom.

So, when dealing with journalists, activists are often in the position not only of holding back from pressing these kinds of critiques, but actually of accepting for strategic purposes the journalists' own understanding of what they do. Here, I return to my claim that most journalists practice their trade in good faith and want to give readers important information. But they don't want to have an argument about political economy and ideology every time they talk to us. And they don't want to be told that no matter how independent they think they are, they are really doing the bidding of owners and managers of the state-corporate-military nexus.

That means that no matter how problematic the concepts of objectivity, neutrality, balance, and fairness, activists have to use them in trying to win space for stories and op/eds that put forth radical ideas. In the chapters that describe specific strategies, I will talk in more detail about how to do this. But the general question from activists to editors should always be, "How can you claim to be objective, neutral, balanced, and fair when you routinely exclude certain political perspectives?" A sharp editor would respond: "We exclude certain perspectives all the time. We don't, for example, give Ku Klux Klan members op/ed space to put forth racist views." At that point, the question is what counts as a credible political perspective. In a world in which radical analysis is seen by many to be discredited and well beyond the spectrum of reasonable opinion, it is our job to present the analysis is a way that makes it difficult for editors to reject out of hand. More on that in the next chapter.

What's Wrong with Objectivity?

After having one unsolicited op/ed accepted by *Newsday*, the daily paper on Long Island, an editor there commissioned me to write something that might help explain why readers are so often fed up with the news. The working hypothesis was that contemporary news is full of too many contradictions, leaving readers hesitant to trust any story because of the chance that the story the next day might say something completely different.

I agreed with the assessment but tried to push the piece more toward the structural and institutional analysis described previously, focusing on the limitations of the craft's objectivity norms.

The piece is critical but hopeful, as are all the essays that are to come in this book.

———————

Journalists actually need less objectivity
Newsday, October 11, 2000, p. A-41

It's not difficult to understand why readers and listeners get frustrated with the news.

One day reports say experts predict that global warming will melt the polar ice caps and flood the world's coastlines. The next day the story is that other experts say there is no global warming; go ahead and buy beach property.

Follow-up stories report that the ice is melting, but it doesn't matter because we'll figure out a way to fix it. Maybe. There are a lot of conflicting, and often jumbled, news reports that float by us every day.

As the public struggles to make sense of the news, it's not surprising that it beats up on journalists for their sins. There is more than enough ignorance, pride and sloth to go around in newsrooms, but the public most often lands on one critique: Journalists are biased. Most often its claim is that the bias is left-wing, an assertion that suffers from only one major problem—a complete lack of evidence to back it up.

The real problem is that reporters aren't biased enough, honestly. The journalistic norms of neutrality and objectivity so constrain reporting that much of the news ends up seeming—or actually being—contradictory or incoherent. The solution: We need journalism that is more biased to help readers get at the truth.

In this sense, biased just means honest. It doesn't mean that journalists should be slavishly partisan or paid agents for one party, group or cause. Nor should journalists ignore facts so they can write a story to fit their personal politics. Instead, journalists should be biased toward the frameworks of analysis that emerge from honest and engaged reporting, on the powerless as well as the powerful. Instead of saying, "We have no opinions," journalists could say, "Listen, we've spent time studying this, and it seems pretty clear to us that the world works this way, and that's the framework we're using to report."

Too much contemporary journalism simply reproduces the worldview of people with power. If news media bosses would give journalists the latitude to be honestly biased, journalists would be a lot happier and write better stories, and the public would have some basis for critically evaluating the news, instead of being asked to pretend that it is all objective.

Take two examples, one technical and one ideological; one contemporary and one historical.

When reporting on the question of global warming, journalists often adopt the dueling-experts format: Some scientists think the warming is happening and is a serious problem, while others disagree. Readers are left to fend for themselves, without the background or expertise to evaluate the claims.

The problem is that most reputable climatologists agree that the warming rate is of serious concern, and that it is primarily the result of human activity. What disagreements exist are mostly about details, not about the existence of the phenomenon or its importance. Most journalists who write about the issue are well aware of this fact. But the news industry's obsession with "balanced" reporting leads to stories that misrepresent the science and mislead the public.

Some reporting problems are more about ideology. Take the Vietnam War, which many Americans still believe the United States lost, in part, because of journalists who were hostile to the U.S. government. In reality, the vast majority of American journalists accepted the government's basic policy goals; it was a lack of truly critical analysis that sent their reporting off the rails.

The coverage would have been far different if U.S. reporters had been ideologically free to report the obvious fact that American planners resisted a political settlement of the war and waged it because they knew that opponents of the Saigon government would run away with any free election—a fact admitted even by President Dwight Eisenhower in his memoirs.

If journalists could have openly offered that framework of analysis, instead of toeing Washington's line, then reporting on the problems of the U.S. war effort would have been more intelligible to the reading public. The U.S. military failures that the press did describe would have made more sense in the context of an honest account of the political situation in Vietnam.

When such contradictory and incomplete reporting is the norm, it's hardly surprising that readers don't trust the press. Journalists mistakenly think the path to credibility is to play the neutrality and objectivity game even more severely, but it's not working. Journalists—and the folks who pay their salaries and run the game—need to realize that credibility will follow from telling the truth, not only about the world around us but about journalism itself.

Are the Media Antibusiness?

For years I had been arguing against the commonly held notion that journalists are antibusiness. The critique of the allegedly antibusiness press ranges from the assertion that reporters simply are too hard on businesspeople to the more bizarre claim that most reporters are raving socialists bent on fomenting world revolution. In all my time in newsrooms, I only met one reporter who called himself a socialist, and he kept it mostly to himself out of fear of retribution. When he told me, it was with the understanding I wouldn't repeat it to our editors.

Throughout the 1990s, as the capitalist triumphalism sparked by the demise of the Soviet Union largely went unchallenged and billionaires became American heroes celebrated by the media, I got increasingly cranky when folks complained to me about how antibusiness the press was. That's when I wrote this essay, comparing the claim that the press is antibusiness to the notion that the press could be antisports. It ran not in the mainstream press but in a specialized magazine about media ethics that is read mostly by academics. After it was published, Michael Albert distributed it on the ZNet commentary email list, which is a part of the alternative information network anchored by Z *Magazine* and the ZNet Web site (www.zmag.org).

The sport of business/the business of sport
Media Ethics, Vol. 11, No. 2, Spring 2000, pp. 4, 20-21

It is often asserted by conservatives, and widely taken as a fact by the general public, that the American news media are "antibusiness." It's a rather silly claim, given the capitalist/managerial framework in which U.S. journalists work, but it is understandable why rightwingers ride the claim for its propaganda value in this very business-run society.

More surprising is that many journalists believe their reporting is highly critical of business. While they would reject the label "antibusiness," many do see themselves and their ethical responsibilities as being tough on business. In this essay, I want to point out just how impoverished that analysis is by using an analogy to sports reporting. Through this issue we can see one of the most serious moral failings of the contemporary news media—the inability to challenge the centralized power of corporate capitalism.

Let's start with that conservative critique, which tends to go something like this: Journalists come in two political shades, liberal and communist. The people who now run newsrooms cut their teeth on the radicalism of the 1960s and hate business. So, journalists unfairly and unethically take every opportunity to bash corporations and the hard-working folks who run them.

This is, on the surface, an odd claim, given that the news media are themselves corporations. It is not clear why the people who own the American media would hire and promote employees who have dedicated themselves to the destruction of the system that enriches them. Despite this obvious problem with the argument, conservatives continue to claim that journalists are antibusiness.

While there is some truth to one element of the claim—that is, journalists can sometimes be mean to businesspeople, just as they can be mean to politicians, celebrities, and others—these critics miss the bigger picture and, therefore, end up with a ludicrous conclusion. Journalists are not antibusiness. They are probusiness, not because of their own political inclinations but because of the values of the system in which they work. For some reason, many people have trouble accepting this elementary point. An analogy to sports journalists, where ideology is not so rigidly imposed and it is easier to see the way the system works, might help.

Sports and business are in many ways similar in American news media (I'm talking specifically about newspapers, though most of this essay applies to radio and television as well). Each has its own section in the newspaper, and news concerning each sometimes spills over into the main news section of the paper. Each has reporters assigned to the section, though general news reporters sometimes cover related stories.

So, let's start by thinking about the day-to-day content of the sports section. Much of the section is devoted to statistics and standings, the data fans want in order to track their specific interests. There also is coverage of the day's events—stories about the personalities, games, and matches that make up the guts of the section. The paper also runs think pieces and trend stories about various sports and the nature of sport. And, finally, there are columnists who are given a fair amount of latitude to spout off about whatever they please.

On any given day, in various parts of the section, there is likely to be criticism of sports—of the league officials, owners, or specific players who have committed various kinds of sins against the fans and the higher ideals of sport. Sports writers, especially columnists, can be among the most vicious in a newsroom, relentlessly going after their targets—including the rich and powerful—with venom and glee. It would be ridiculous, however, to claim that sports writers are antisports. They live and breathe a sports culture. They write for a section devoted solely to that culture. They are subsidized in their work by the very industry they cover (through press boxes, free food, easy access to information, etc.). They are, without exception in my experience, sports lovers. And, of course, readers and critics understand this. When disgruntled readers argue with sports columnists, they don't accuse them of being antisports. They simply say, "You're a jerk—you're wrong about that."

Much the same can be said of newspapers' business coverage. The business section includes lots of statistics and data (stock tables, etc.) and daily coverage of personalities, companies, and deal-making. There is coverage of the business world's daily events (which corporations bought what, what earnings or new products are anticipated, which CEO has quit, etc.), along with think pieces and trend stories. Some of the stories can be critical of specific corporations or individual owners. Some of the criticism can be annoying to the just-fired CEO, or the company that would rather have the public (and peers) kept in the dark about some of its problems. It can even be harsh, especially when a corporation has given all business a bad name by egregiously ripping off clients or consumers—although no business reporter or columnist ever writes with the viciousness of a sports writer. Likewise, business reporters tend to live and breathe business culture. They write for a section devoted solely to that culture. They are subsidized in their work by the entities they cover through a huge PR industry that provides free "information" on a massive scale. They are, without exception in my experience, business lovers.

And, just as the sports reporter almost never steps back and asks, "Just what is going on with sports in this culture—what's the big picture?" so too the business reporter almost never steps back and asks, "Just what is going on with capitalism in this culture—what's the big picture?" Sports reporters and business reporters are not critics of the system; at best, they police its boundaries. They report on violations of the rules; they don't ask questions about the fundamental justice of the rules. To varying degrees, we all understand this about sports reporters, which is why no one would ever think to label them antisports. This probably is because sports, in some sense, doesn't much matter—it's just children's games being played by adults, albeit games that generate incredible profits and take a lot of our time. In many ways, sports supports the ideology of the culture, both in the values it promotes—aggressive competitiveness and a focus on winning—and in its equally important role in producing a passive, depoliticized population. But sports is not at the core of the culture's ideology. Capitalism is.

Everyone understands the central importance to their well-being of how an economy is structured. Throughout the past two centuries, many people have realized that capitalism, especially in its increasingly concentrated corporate form, is detrimental to their well-being. People have been murdered, gone to jail, and been exiled in a struggle to resist the injustice of that economic system. Even though it may seem that, in the post-Cold War era, capitalism has "won," smart capitalists understand that victory is always tentative. Today, working people and the unions that once created a channel for working people's power are on the defensive, but thoughtful capitalists know how quickly that can change. Hence the need for intense ideological control and indoctrination.

My own view is that the overtly reactionary publishers and editors who clamp down on any critical reporting, and the right-wing think tanks that attack even mild attempts at critique, are actually working against their own purposes. As corporate America continues to put the screws to Americans, even the most indoctrinated (take, for example, the working-class people who might truly believe that lowering the capital gains tax will create benefits that trickle down to them) will see that the system is stacked against them. And if the picture that the media paint of business is so overwhelmingly positive that it cannot possibly be made to jibe with the experiences of working people, such coverage actually will begin to work against business: The propaganda will be so out of sync with people's experiences that it will become less effective. (This often happens, for example, on many large university campuses, where administrators talk about being "student-centered" and students, who daily encounter a bureaucracy that has no concern for them, don't even bother to laugh; they know it is meaningless PR talk.)

In fact, having a business press as feisty as the sports press (while always, of course, staying within the bounds of unquestioned support for the fundamental system), would probably in the long run work in favor of business. The appearance of serious criticism might help preserve the illusion of a democratic society.

All this leaves journalists in a tough spot. Reflexively, they want to deny being antibusiness because the ideology of objectivity precludes them from being pro- or anti- anything. At the same time, journalists often think of themselves as doing tough reporting on business. But, as I have argued above, while journalists police the most visible, egregious violations of the rules, they rarely question the rules themselves. Their tough reporting can land a corrupt CEO in jail or result in a company being fined for an environmental infraction, but it doesn't highlight the basic questions about why we have allowed corporations to acquire so much power and how the routine exercise of that power creates and entrenches inequality. The ethical challenge for reporters is to make good on the watchdog function they claim is central to the profession. The key question is, watching what or whom? Journalists tend to see themselves as primarily watching government, which historically has had the most power to abuse people in our society. In limited ways, reporters do occasionally fulfill that role, though in certain arenas (most notably foreign policy), reporters almost never challenge policymakers.

We need to ask, where does real power in this society lie? Where or who else should journalists be watching? The answer, clearly, is where power is most concentrated, which is in the corporations. That means not only reporting on individual corporations, but reporting on the nature of the corporate system—the ever-increasing power of corporations and the way they constrain ordinary people's lives, both at home and abroad. Right now, in an age of capitalist triumphalism, journalism has failed miserably at that task. Rather than challenging corporate power, news outlets routinely trumpet the great accomplishments of owners and managers. Claims about the inevitability and universal benefit of markets go uncritiqued. Articulate opponents of so-called "free" trade are treated as cranks. And the inherently antidemocratic nature of corporations (which are, after all, internally structured as top-down hierarchies with no pretense of democracy) cannot be mentioned in polite company.

Journalists have a moral choice to subordinate themselves to corporate power or to challenge it. The institutional structure is set up for subordination; as in other institutions in the culture, there are obvious rewards that come with following power. But journalism is not yet so completely locked down that good work can't be done. It takes creativity, ingenuity, and courage. The rewards rarely come in terms of money or career advancement. But neither does one have to wait for the afterlife for the reward of knowing that in the struggle of haves and have-nots, one made the right choice.

Chapter 3

Making Sense of a
Complex World in 700 Words

Although many people find it hard to believe, one can write a coherent radical argument in 700 words. It is hard work, and invariably one has to leave out evidence and reasoning that can make the case more compelling to folks with opposing views. But a lot can be done in such a small space. This chapter will set out some basic tips before moving to more specific strategies in the rest of the book.

I start with some notes about terminology. It is important to understand how journalists refer to various kinds of writing in the newspaper and to use the terms properly; knowing their language conveys to them that you took the time to understand how they work. First, the term "editorial" is used in different ways, depending on context. It sometimes is used to describe all the nonadvertising material in the paper; journalists will talk about "editorial content" as opposed to "advertising content," or the "editorial side" versus the "advertising side" of the operation. But in other contexts, editorial (where writers can openly express opinions) is distinguished from news (where reporters are not supposed to express opinions openly). Even though few readers believe that the distinction is all that meaningful, remember we are playing by the journalists' rules here.

Most daily newspapers have two pages for opinion writing, most often called the editorial page and the op/ed page. Typically the editorial page contains several short, unsigned pieces that are presented as the institutional voice of the paper. These are what journalists call an editorial. This page usually also contains an editorial cartoon and letters to the editor—the short (usually no more than 200 words) responses from readers to articles in the paper.

"Op/ed" stands for "opposite the editorial page" and is used to describe the opinion pieces that are on the page facing the newspaper's editorials. It is also sometimes used in the sense of "opinion and editorials," to indicate that whole section of paper. Three general types of articles run on the op/ed page: syndicated columns, signed columns by newspaper staff members, and pieces by people outside the newspaper. Those pieces that come from syndicated and staff writers are commonly referred to as "columns," while the pieces by nonstaff are usually called "op/eds," which run from 400 to 800 words.

When talking to editors, use the terms in these ways to convey an understanding of the process and to avoid confusion. Don't tell an editor you want to submit an editorial; call it an op/ed. If you are responding to an article that ran in the paper, realize that the editor will probably want to run a response as a letter to the editor, though sometimes a paper will give op/ed space to someone for a response. If you have an idea for an original article/essay, say you want to submit an op/ed.

Although one gets more space to develop an idea in an op/ed, the briefer letters can sometimes be easier to get published and more effective (the letters section is one of the best-read parts of a paper). Most editors feel an obligation to run critiques of stories that have appeared in their paper, though they won't (and can't because of space limitations) run every letter they get. But getting your letter published is not the only measure of success; often a deluge of letters will force editors to publish a representative sample, and your unpublished letter could be part of that critical mass. Also remember that most papers won't accept a letter on behalf of a group; an individual has to sign it. Some papers also have a limit on how many letters they will publish from one person (often one a month).

Journalistic Style

One of the most difficult things for nonjournalists to do is to adopt the style of journalism. Many people learned to write in other genres that allow more room to develop an argument. Journalists generally don't have that luxury. Two general points about writing op/eds are crucial: (1) don't try to accomplish too much in one piece, and (2) learn to be merciless in editing yourself, in cutting unnecessary words and phrases. An effective op/ed is not so much a product of writing but of rewriting and editing.

On the first point: Remember the newspaper readers do not always devote lots of time or serious attention to any one article. To be effective, writers have to make their arguments clear immediately. If readers are two or three paragraphs into a piece and don't yet understand the main point, it is unlikely they will continue. The thinking behind an op/ed should be complex, but the piece itself should be simple.

Much the same thing can be said about evidence used in a piece. Writers need to back up claims, but it has to be done in abbreviated fashion; one has to convey that there is considerable evidence behind the argument but that it simply can't be offered in this format. This is difficult enough when writing from a mainstream point of view (when one can draw on the conventional wisdom that most people accept without thinking), but even harder when trying to fashion an op/ed that puts forth a radical view. For example, during the Cold War, writers could simply mention "the Soviet threat" without ever supplying evidence of the nature of the threat. Radicals arguing against U.S. policy based on Cold War rationales would have to spend time taking apart such hackneyed justifications.

On style: The best way to figure out how to write like a journalist is to read the paper. Journalistic writing is not a terribly complex form, and a serious reader of the paper can pick up most of it without too much trouble. Some points are obvious: avoid flowery language, write in clear and concise fashion, keep paragraphs to no more than one or two sentences. But beyond that, one has to learn to be ruthless in editing oneself. The unnecessary words you cut out give you more room to bolster the argument with evidence and clear reasoning. There are lots of writing books that help with this. One of the best on explaining how to edit oneself is William Zinsser's *On Writing Well*. For guidance on technical questions—journalist's style on things such as punctuation, abbreviations, word usage—the *Associated Press Stylebook* is the definitive source and worth the investment.

Beyond structure and style, one of the key questions concerns how radical one can be and still get published. The answer depends in part on the specific editor to whom you are sending the piece. If the decision-making editor on the op/ed page is a right-wing fanatic, radical pieces may be impossible to place there. But even those kinds of ideologues sometimes run pieces critical of their positions out of a belief in balance. True, they may run 25 right-wing pieces for every radical piece, but that one radical piece could be yours. Most editors, even those who are conservative, make good-faith attempts to produce a page with some diversity of opinion. They take seriously their charge to be a reflection of the thinking of the public, or at least "respectable" segments of the public. Editors also like controversial pieces that stir up readers and generate letters to the editor. The task is to make editors understand that your views—no matter how radical—are not flaky and idiosyncratic, but represent a constituency.

To do that, it is crucial that your op/ed not sound like it was written by the central committee of The Party (whatever party that may be). Take care to avoid phrases that will be seen as left-wing clichés. Instead of talking about "worker control of the means of production," talk about how workers should be able to make decisions about their own lives and work. Even if you think Marx proved a point, don't write, "As Marx showed us..." I offer this advice not to denigrate but to be realistic; mainstream editors are turned off by anything that smacks of ideological fanaticism on the left (the right can, and does sound, as fanatical as it likes—it's not a fair world).

Journalistic writing at its best is punchy and relaxed. Success-ful writers realize that readers are sitting down with the newspa-per in varied situations and often have a lot of competition for their attention. Successful writing grabs readers and carries them along while providing important information and analysis. "Seri-ous" writers often denigrate journalistic writing, sometimes for good reason—journalism is far too often shallow, uninteresting, formulaic, and irrelevant. But it doesn't have to be; the craft need not be practiced that way.

Working with Editors

Personal contact with editors is important, but remember that journalists are generally overworked. Like any relationship in which one person has more control and authority, it is a fine line between being persistent and being harassing. Persistence can pay off, but when editors feel harassed they are less likely to run anything you write. Here's a sensible approach:

Most newspapers have Web sites, and most sites have staff directories and/or instructions for how to submit letters and opinion pieces. Some papers also run this information on the op/ed pages. If you can't find that information, call and talk to a receptionist or clerk and figure out who has decision-making authority. At larger papers, there usually are lower-level editors or clerks who are responsible for receiving and tracking submissions, while someone higher up makes the actual decision. On the largest papers, there generally is an editor of the editorial pages who has several deputies who do much of the daily work.

Most papers now accept submissions via email, which is generally easier for editors because they don't have to have submissions retyped. Faxes are usually accepted as well. You can send a piece in regular mail, but timeliness usually makes that a bad route. Whenever possible, get the name of the specific editor or editors who handle op/eds. It is always better to contact a person by name than by addressing something to "editor in charge of op/eds." Make sure you include your complete contact information: full name, group affiliation if relevant, mailing address, phone and fax numbers at home and work, and email address.

One important question to ask is the newspaper's policy on multiple submissions. When you are writing about a purely local issue or responding directly to a story from that paper, you likely will submit the piece to that paper only. But many op/eds about national and international issues could run in any paper in the country. Most papers request that you give them the right to run the piece first in their circulation area and don't care if you also try to sell the piece elsewhere. But larger papers (the *New York Times*, *Washington Post*, and *Los Angeles Times*, for example) demand first-rights nationally—if you sell your piece to them, you can't offer it to other papers until after they have run it. At all papers I have ever dealt with, the newspaper buys one-time rights to your piece (usually for both print and electronic uses, to cover use on Web sites and in databases) and copyright reverts to the writer after that. That means you control subsequent uses of the piece. If you don't know a paper's policy, be sure to ask.

You can call editors before you have written a piece to find out if they are interested in the topic. Sometimes that call can save you work; if the paper has run what the editor thinks is too many pieces on a subject already, she/he might be honest and say there's no point in you submitting a similar piece. But the standard response to "Would you be interested in a piece on X?" is "Sure, we are always looking for material from local writers, but we can't guarantee we will run it."

After submitting a piece, a simple way to establish personal contact with an editor is to call and verify that the piece arrived. It is a legitimate question; emails sometimes get lost in hard-drive crashes, and faxes don't always get delivered to the right person. That short conversation also fixes in the editor's mind that there is a real person with a voice behind the op/ed. As long as one doesn't call on deadline late in the day and doesn't draw out the conversation if the editor is busy, there's little risk in making that kind of call.

Once accepted, your op/ed will be edited. At some papers, especially smaller ones that are understaffed, that might mean little more than a copy editor running spell-check on the piece. But sometimes the editing will be more extensive, either for reasons of style, space, or politics. I rarely fight a change an editor wants to make for style, even if I disagree with the need for it, unless the change seriously disrupts the argument I am trying to make in the piece. When it's a matter of space, all one can do is help the editor find the cuts that do the least damage to the piece (that's if the editor engages you in the process; not all will). If there are disputes about politics and an editor tells you "you can't say that," you can negotiate, but remember that the writer generally has less power. You may have to accept changes to get the piece published, which forces you to judge whether the changes so distort the point you want to make as to render the piece useless. Writers always can play their final card—"publish it my way or I will pull the piece"—but that works only if the editor really wants to use the piece.

In my experience, overtly politicized editing is rare. It is likely that many pieces are rejected because editors don't like the radical politics of a piece, but once they accept an op/ed editors rarely attempt to destroy a piece through editing. In the dozens of op/eds I have published in the past few years, I sometimes have been edited for space. But I know of only one change that was made because of politics. A lower-level editor confided to me that the editor of the editorial pages, who disagreed with the position I took in the piece, said he would allow it to be published only if a phrase were taken out. The change was unnecessary and annoying to me, but not serious enough for me to throw a fit. So, I let the piece run as edited.

Writing op/eds is like any other freelance writing—it's frustrating and requires patience. Unless you have a piece that the whole world is waiting to read, you are always at the mercy of the editor. If your calls aren't returned promptly or email goes unanswered, don't take it personally. It is part of the game. Persistence usually pays off. But this means you have to accept that every piece you write will not get published. It means sometimes smiling at an editor you think is a buffoon. It means accepting editing you don't like. In that sense, it is no different than any other political activity—most successes require compromise.

PART II
WRITING STRATEGIES AND EXAMPLES

Chapter 4

Today's Headlines

In some sense, all op/eds have to connect up with the news. If you submit a treatise on Central Asian art of the sixteenth century, editors will ask the obvious question: "Who cares? We run a *news*paper—how does the piece relate to issues in the news? Why would readers be interested?" On occasions, editors will run pieces that are simply ruminations on the state of the world, and some papers like to drop in an occasional humor piece. But in the vast majority of cases, op/eds have to have what journalists call a news hook or peg—the central point of the op/ed has to relate to an issue, personality, or trend that is deemed newsworthy.

This chapter includes the most basic kind of op/eds—pieces that offer commentary directly about an event or issue from the daily headlines. In these cases, the keys to getting published are timeliness and distinctiveness.

Timeliness is always cited as one of the criteria for determining what is news. Reporters and editors often tell each other and the public that an item is inappropriate for the paper because the news is more than a day or two old. But like the other criteria, timeliness is flexible, and editors will allow into the paper stories about "old news" if they have a reason (specific strategies for such cases are covered in subsequent chapters).

Still, timeliness remains one of the most common reasons that an editor will reject an op/ed. If an issue was in the news on Monday and you don't submit the op/ed until the next week, two outcomes are likely. Either someone else will have beaten you to the punch or, even if the paper hasn't run something about the issue, it will be seen as outdated.

Luckily, op/ed editors don't have to work on as strict a sense of timeliness as the news reporters, who literally often will discard some stories if they are more than 24 hours old. Because the op/ed page is seen as a place for a deeper reflection on important questions, an issue can be a couple of days old—sometimes even a couple of weeks old—and still be seen as relevant. And some ongoing stories provide multiple opportunities for op/eds, as a bill moves through different stages in Congress, for example. But competition for space always argues for getting a piece to an editor as quickly as possible.

Just as important is distinctiveness. Op/ed editors usually have access to a large number of syndicated columns about national and international issues, and even on local issues there often are many folks offering up op/eds. Editors are looking for pieces from local writers that don't say exactly the same thing as what they have read on the wires. In this regard, radical writers actually have an edge, because there are no syndicated columns by truly radical folks; there are a few progressive/populist columnists, but they don't consistently offer a radical voice. Jumping on a topic in the news with a radical analysis that is rarely heard in the mainstream can be effective.

World Trade Organization

The Seattle WTO meeting is a good example of how this works. Although much of the country was caught off guard by the massive protest in Seattle, radicals around the country—at least those of us who were plugged into the organizing network and were constantly receiving email about protest plans—knew what was coming. I began thinking about how to use the news event to publish a critique of the WTO and the corporate globalization rhetoric well in advance. I collected information and thought through what my main points would be, but I wasn't sure of how to frame the piece until shortly before the meeting.

I waited to make that decision because I knew there would be a lot of discussion on op/ed pages about the issue. I'm not an economist or business expert; I knew I had no special leverage to wedge myself into the paper. So, I waited for an opening.

That opening came when I read a story that quoted U.S. Trade Representative Charlene Barshefsky on the problem officials faced: a lack of public support. Every now and then important people say really stupid things that reveal what their real agenda is—in this case to ram through procorporate globalization policies over public opposition. Most of us know that is the case, but when someone such as Barshefsky acknowledges that the public is often an obstacle to elite decisionmakers' real goals, it is a great opportunity to point out the hypocrisy.

As the opening of the WTO talks neared and protesters from around the world streamed into Seattle, even the mainstream media began to realize how big the story would be. So, when I read Barshefsky's comments on a Sunday and began to think about how to write the piece, I was relatively confident that editors would be interested. I wrote the piece Sunday night, rewrote and polished on Monday morning. I knew that if I got the piece in that morning, editors could read it in time to consider it for the Tuesday paper, the day the meeting—and protest.

On this one, I got lucky. The op/ed page editor at the *Houston Chronicle* had run a couple of my pieces before this, and I had built up some capital there. I suspect that is why he opened my email fairly quickly after receiving it and was willing to consider my piece instead of the other WTO op/eds that were available to him that day. The combination of being there at the right time, with a slightly different take on the issue (not the minutia of trade policy, but a focus on the fundamental issue of democracy), did the trick, and the piece ran on N30, as the day was called by activists.

As a footnote, this case should remind us that there are many different ways to contribute to a political movement. I had very much wanted to go to Seattle for the protest, to be where the main action was going to be. My work and travel schedule made it impossible, but even if that hadn't been the case I likely would have stayed in Austin, where we held a local demonstration to coincide with what was happening in Seattle. It's also unlikely that I would have gotten the op/ed published if I had traveled to Seattle. I could have lugged my laptop with me, but there wouldn't have been the time to sit down and carefully compose the piece that ran.

Let ordinary folks shut down WTO decision-makers' tent
Houston Chronicle, November 30, 1999, p. 27-A

It is a strange democracy when a high government official can chastise the public for not holding the right opinion. But consider

the remarks of U.S. Trade Representative Charlene Barshefsky on
the public protests of the World Trade Organization meeting in
Seattle: "Not to move forward on those issues puts the global
trading system at peril," she said, "because the biggest threat to
open markets is the lack of public support."

If we understood democracy actually to mean rule by the people, then a lack of public support for a policy should make officials stop and consider the wisdom of the policy. But Barshefsky
and others in the Clinton administration have no time for such
idealistic notions of the relevance of citizen concerns. Instead, they
are worried that an outbreak of democracy could derail plans to
solidify corporate control over the world's economy at this week's
WTO meeting.

And make no mistake, that is exactly what is on the table in
Seattle, which is why people are taking to the streets by the thousands around the country to express their displeasure at the attempts to shove corporate domination down the throats of regular
folks. Ordinary citizens quite clearly are telling the administration
that we won't buy the empty rhetoric about free trade and open
markets, and that we want fair trade and an economic system that
serves the needs of people, not corporations.

The WTO was created in 1995 out of the "Uruguay Round" of
the General Agreement on Tariffs and Trade. The 135 member
countries agree to abide by the WTO's rules, which go far beyond
tariffs to address "nontariff barriers to trade" in an attempt to
deregulate international commerce and force open domestic markets to foreign investment. In short, the WTO strengthens the
power of corporations and weakens the ability of governments to
protect workers and the environment.

Under WTO rules, countries can challenge each others' laws
and regulations as barriers to trade. When a country loses at the
WTO, it can change laws to conform to the WTO requirements,
pay compensation to the other country, or have nonnegotiated
trade sanctions forced on it. A panel of three trade bureaucrats
decides the cases, and in the first four years those decisions have
gone for the corporations and against workers, public health and
the environment.

So, the WTO is an attack on democracy because nonelected
power brokers constrain the actions of democratically elected

governments. That attack is even more dramatic because the WTO tribunals operate in secret; proceedings and documents are confidential, with no right to outside appeals. In the United States, this will undermine environmental regulations and hamper the efforts of working people to organize for better pay and working conditions.

But the people who really will suffer will be in the Third World. WTO regulations will force open even more dramatically the markets of Third World countries to the multinational corporations from rich countries. The policies often demanded of these countries by the International Monetary Fund and World Bank— slashing social spending and accommodating foreign investors— will be intensified under WTO rule. That means a continued erosion of basic health and human services in those countries, while governments also will be thwarted in attempts to protect domestic industries and agriculture.

All this is justified by the unsupported claim that "free trade" benefits everyone. Never mind that even a cursory look at history shows that every advanced economy, including the United States', was built not on free trade but protectionism. Never mind that only when rich nations have great advantages do they sing the praises of free trade.

As economist Robin Hahnel points out in his new book *Panic Rules!*, increases in trade and international investment do not necessarily produce efficiency gains. And when they do, they almost always aggravate the already profound and immoral inequalities within countries and between rich and poor countries.

How does the administration answer these citizen concerns? Clinton offers to "bring inside the tent" the dissident voices. But the goal of the movement against corporate-sponsored globalization is not to come into the tent for Clinton's dog-and-pony show. We're saying that it is time to shut this tent down.

The question is not globalization, about whether or not we all now are connected in new ways brought about by changes in politics, economics, and technology. The question is, on what values will a global economy be based? The inherent dignity of all people to live meaningful lives of their own choosing, or the rights of corporations to make those choices in the quest of ever-higher profits?

In a democracy, those choices are made by the people, in the people's tent. Not by Clinton, Barshefsky and the rest of the bought-and-paid-for barkers in the corporate tent.

Africa Trade Bill

This op/ed is an example of how not being an expert should not stop us from writing. Much legislation in a complex society is difficult for ordinary citizens to understand, let alone master. But that doesn't mean that ordinary citizens can't figure things out and write about them in a way that other regular folks can grasp.

This piece grew out of local organizing around global trade issues. Soon after the Multilateral Agreement on Investments (MAI) was derailed, many of us who had just gotten involved in such issues realized there was more to it than the MAI. In the time between the MAI and the WTO efforts, one of the issues that got our attention was Africa. I had no more expertise on the issue than anyone else in the group, but I volunteered for op/ed duty when we divided up chores.

There is no original research or analysis in this piece. I did a quick database search for articles on the issue and then visited several of the many good Web sites of activist groups on trade issues, collecting facts and comparing groups' analyses. From there, I tried to distill the key pieces of information that people would need to make sense of the issue and to present it in a way that cut through the facile claims made about free markets and free trade. The economic situation in Africa is so unfamiliar to most Americans that I assumed readers would have absolutely no prior knowledge, which argued for keeping the piece even more simple than usual.

Although I am never scared to write about things in which I have no claim to special knowledge, in this case my lack of background on Africa led me to seek help and a coauthor. A colleague in the University of Texas history department was willing to supply the help and sign on as a coauthor. Robin Kilson helped hone the piece, and no doubt the presence of her name on the byline made the piece more attractive (history carries more prestige than journalism behind a professor's name).

This piece does not seem particularly radical on the surface. It engages a debate about legislation, rarely the site of radical politics. This is a case in which there were multiple goals in writing. We wanted both to influence the outcome of the debate over the bill (a failed project; the bad bill ended up being passed) and to push a more basic point about the way in which all the trade talk is framed to benefit large corporations, not people. The piece doesn't call for the overthrow of capitalism, but that doesn't mean its argument for one trade bill over another is not rooted in radical politics.

Africa needs HOPE, not exploitation
San Antonio Express-News, March 9, 1999, p. 7B

by Robin Kilson and Robert Jensen

In a world where even the experts don't seem to understand very much about how global trade and finance really work, it can be a daunting task for ordinary citizens to sort through complex trade proposals.

The questions about the African Growth and Opportunity Act—dubbed the "NAFTA for Africa" bill by critics who fear it will gut the African economy just as NAFTA has done to the Mexican economy—seem even more complex, given that people in the African-American community are lining up on both sides. U.S. Rep. Jesse Jackson Jr. and the respected black-studies scholar Cornel West are against it; on the other side are the Rev. Jesse Jackson and NAACP President Kweisi Mfume. The Congressional Black Caucus is split on the issue.

One place to start to make sense of the bill is to ask some questions not just about who supports the bill—after all, reasonable people of common faith and principle can disagree about political strategy—but about who stands to gain from the policy. One doesn't need a degree in international finance to understand that the megacorporations lining up to push the bill aren't doing it out of concern for Africa and Africans, but to line their pockets with megaprofits that the bill will make possible.

Those profits will be squeezed out of countries that could benefit from a bill that truly was about economic growth and opportunity. Instead, this trade agreement would in the short term increase the suffering on that continent and could be a long-term economic disaster. It promises not real development, but the "recolonization of Africa," as one African critic has put it.

What's wrong with the bill? Rather than benefit African nations, it will force them to open up their economies to multinational corporations; reduce corporate taxes and cut spending on health, education, and food subsidies; and sell off Africa's enormous natural resources to private individuals and corporations. To see how that works, all you have to do is look at how similar International Monetary Fund policies already in place have reduced the standard of living for Africans.

If they accept those conditions, African nations will be eligible for benefits in the bill, but even those benefits are largely illusory. The bill promises additional access into the U.S. market for textiles and apparel, but those quotas end in 2004. Other "benefits," such as granting least-developed-country status, are already in place for most of the sub-Saharan countries.

The almost-certain result of the bill: African economies would be opened up to "development" (meaning, "exploitation") by multinational corporations, while African countries would be handicapped by a severe shortage of capital, much of which goes to pay off the existing debt. If they are going to develop, African countries need the same power that the United States and Europe had when they started—the ability to protect their own economies and set their own policies. The bill robs African countries of this freedom, all in the name of mythical free-trade policies that the great powers have never accepted for themselves.

Opponents of the bill aren't trying to block real economic development in Africa and have put forth proposals for an alternative bill that does more than enrich corporations. A key to any plan must be debt relief; development in Africa is impossible with 80 percent of all export earnings now earmarked for debt payment. The United States and other developed nations also have a moral obligation to offer aid to overcome the damage of past exploitation of the continent. The goal should be self-determination through trade and investment rules that benefit people and regulate corporate excesses. The current bill does the opposite, constraining people and freeing up corporations.

So, the first and most pressing step is to kill the African Growth and Opportunity Act being sponsored by Rep. Charles Rangel (D-N.Y.). As TransAfrica's president Randall Robinson puts it, "A bad bill on Africa is worse than no bill at all."

The next step is to promote the alternative bill sponsored by U.S. Rep. Jesse Jackson Jr. (D-Ill.). The HOPE (Human Rights, Opportunity, Partnership and Empowerment) for Africa Act will cancel the debt owed by African countries to the U.S. government and take steps to relieve the debt burden to multilateral lending agencies and private lenders. This bill also has important provisions for environmental, worker-safety, labor-rights, and living-wage standards, and will ensure that aid and development money is used for basic social services and strengthening and diversifying Africa's economies.

We must demand that Africa, a continent that has struggled in this century to recover from the devastation of the old colonialism, not be burdened with a new colonialism in the coming century.

Iraq Bombings

This op/ed is an example of how to play off an ongoing story that receives little attention in the mainstream. Since the December 1998 Desert Fox bombings of Iraq, the United States and Britain carried out routine attacks on Iraq that, at most, rated a couple of paragraphs in most newspapers. To mainstream journalists, it was a nonstory.

The piece hangs on the irony of the United States claiming to be upholding international law when it was in fact violating that law. But the main objective in writing it was to highlight the effects of the economic sanctions, which was the focus of much of my local political work then. At that point, the sanctions were not seen as much of a story by editors, and I thought it would be easier to peg the piece to the bombings. Everyone can imagine a bomb dropping and killing people, but the effects of an economic embargo — which in this case has killed far more than the bombs — are harder for people to understand.

In addition to the specific issues, in most everything I write about U.S. foreign policy I try to highlight the inconsistencies and hypocrisy in the rhetoric from U.S. officials. Far too many Americans believe that in world affairs the United States is engaged in some sort of noble quest to bring peace and justice to the world. So, every chance I get I try to make visible the obvious: that U.S. policymakers are motivated by the same self-interest that has motivated other great powers throughout history. Nobility has nothing to do with it. So, when I find outrageous quotes such as the one from Madeline Albright used in this piece, I throw them in a file to use later in pieces such as this.

Ongoing issues such as the bombing of Iraq make good hooks for op/eds because one has more time — there isn't an imperative to get the piece done by the end of the day. That also is the weakness, however; editors can easily decide that there is no imperative to run the piece. I sent this piece to editors all over the country, aware that it was a long shot. I got lucky only with the Palm Beach daily and a weekly paper in Austin.

U.S. a global bully; attacks on Iraq violate law
Palm Beach Post, March 20, 1999, p. 13A

"U.S. jets drop bunker bombs on Iraq."
"Allied warplanes conduct 3 raids in Iraqi no-fly zones."
Day after day, the headlines about air strikes against Iraq appear in the papers, usually followed by explanations of how the United States and Britain are protecting the integrity of the no-fly zones.

One simple fact is routinely missing from these stories: The no-fly zones have no integrity because they are, in fact, illegal, and the U.S./UK air attacks are war crimes.

Despite the best efforts of State Department spin doctors to convince us that the no-fly zones are UN-mandated, these zones

are imposed by the United States and Britain (France once partici-
pated, but has pulled out) with no credible legal authority. There
is not, and has never been, a Security Council resolution that
authorizes any nation to patrol the skies of Iraq after the 1991 Gulf
War. The United States and UK are perpetrating illegal acts of
aggression under international law.

This is all made more sordid by the hypocritical rationale
given: The no-fly zones are there to protect the Kurds in the north
and the Shiites in the south. I doubt that the Shiites who at-
tempted to rise up in 1991 after the war, and were slaughtered by
Saddam Hussein's army under the watchful eye of U.S. forces, are
reassured to know the United States is now their protector. Nor
are the Kurds, who have been used as a political ping-pong ball
by Washington for decades, likely to be bolstered by the news.

It might seem odd that in a free society with a free press, basic
questions about the legality and morality of a policy are almost
never raised. It's worth pondering why reporters do not stand up
at every State Department briefing to ask, "Why does the United
States continue to pursue military solutions that violate international law while rejecting the international consensus that calls for
a less belligerent and more humane approach to Iraq?"

That consensus includes not only an end to the bombings, but
the lifting of the economic sanctions still imposed on Iraq at the
insistence of the United States. The embargo, even with the inadequate oil-for-food plan, continues to kill children at the rate of
about 5,000 a month, according to UN statistics; it's likely that
more than 1 million Iraqis have died since 1991. Still, U.S. officials
continue to talk about sanctions as an alternative to war, even as
the embargo kills far more people than the bombs.

But simple questions are rarely asked. So, Bill Clinton was not
challenged when he explained to the U.S. public in December that
he must bomb Iraq to make sure they comply with UN Security
Council resolutions concerning weapons inspection.

In other words, Clinton asserts that we must violate international law to uphold international law. Just as no Security Council
resolution authorizes the no-fly zones, no resolution authorizes
this use of military force against Iraq. When Clinton let loose the
bombers and missiles in December, he was outside of international law, acting as a terrorist in charge of a rogue state.

The facts of this matter are not complex: The UN charter, the foundational document for international law, provides for military action by one member state against another only when a state is under direct armed attack. In all other situations, nations must first appeal to the Security Council to resolve disputes, and only the Security Council can authorize the use of force.

But nary a mention of these unpleasant facts shows up in the mainstream press or on television news in the United States. The fault lies not so much with individual journalists, but with the ideological framework for reporting on U.S. policy, which takes as a given that the United States has the power, and hence the right, to impose its will on the world, with extreme violence if deemed necessary.

Journalists, it seems, can't see their way clear to challenge Secretary of State Madeline Albright's assertion that "we will act multilaterally when we can, and unilaterally when we must."

That's the equivalent of the neighborhood bully saying "I'll follow the law when I feel like it and ignore the law when I feel like it." Such a posture is not diplomacy, but the antithesis of diplomacy; these are the tactics of thugs, not of a nation that allegedly is based on a commitment to the rule of law.

If the United States is serious about a long-term just peace in the Middle East, this immoral, illegal, and ineffective starve-and-bomb strategy must give way to real diplomacy and compassion for the suffering of real people in Iraq.

Cheney and War Crimes

When Dick Cheney was named George W. Bush's running mate in the summer of 2000, journalists began to pick apart his record, highlighting his more reactionary votes that were seen as out of step with the American mainstream. But no one was talking about his record as secretary of defense during the Gulf War and his responsibility for the barbaric level of destruction Iraqis suffered at the hands of the United States in 1991. I used that climate of reviewing candidates' records to raise the war-crimes question, which otherwise would have been hard to put forward.

This op/ed had two goals. One was to argue to U.S. citizens that the Gulf War, which we are told made Americans feel good about the country's military and vanquished the "Vietnam syndrome," was a sad moment in U.S. history. The second was to bring up again the issue of the devastating effect of the economic embargo on the people of Iraq. The linchpin of this piece was a 1991 *Washington Post* story in which Cheney made it clear he had no second thoughts about the level of destruction.

Although I wrote this piece, the idea for it was not mine. Bert Sacks, an antisanctions activist with Western Washington Fellowship of Reconciliation and Voices in the Wilderness, had noted the Cheney comments and thought they could be the basis for an op/ed. Bert had read some of my work and thought I could do a good job with it. So he contacted me and I went forward with writing the piece. This is another reminder that no matter whose name is on an op/ed or any piece of writing, the process by which that writing came to be is not individual. We come to understand the world as much—if not more—through conversation as solitary thought.

Lingering question: Is Dick Cheney guilty of war crimes against Iraqis?
Fort Worth Star-Telegram, September 5, 2000, p. 11B

There has been much criticism lately of Republican vice-presidential candidate Dick Cheney's business record—the propriety of his stock options, his role in getting government contracts, and whether or not he earned the millions he was paid. Earlier this summer we also heard much about some of Cheney's less compassionate conservative votes in Congress—against gun control, Head Start and Nelson Mandela.

All those issues are relevant and worthy of discussion. But what is striking is that no one is talking about another aspect of the Cheney record—his admission of war crimes in the Gulf War.

Go back to the summer of 1991, after the Gulf War. The results of the 43-day bombing campaign—the most devastating concentrated bombing attack in history—were painfully clear. A Harvard study team had reported that the attack on Iraqi electrical, water, and sewage treatment systems had begun to kill thousands of civilians, especially the most vulnerable—children, the elderly, the sick.

Though international law specifically prohibits civilian targets, Pentagon planners and U.S. politicians knew perfectly well that civilians would die as a result of those bombs. As a *Washington Post* reporter put it after extensive interviews with military officials that summer, some Iraqi infrastructure was bombed primarily to create "postwar leverage." The "damage to civilian structures and interests, invariably described by briefers during the war as 'collateral' and unintended, was sometimes neither," the reporter concluded.

After 10 years of the most comprehensive multilateral economic sanctions in modern times, at least 1 million Iraqis have died as a result, according to UN studies.

So, what did Cheney have to say about these choices of targets after the war, when there was no way to deny the deadly effects on civilians?

Every Iraqi target was "perfectly legitimate," Cheney told the *Post* reporter, adding "if I had to do it over again, I would do exactly the same thing."

Cheney has never repudiated this comment, never expressed contrition for the deaths of innocents that he had to have known would result from policies he helped shape and implement. But instead of being challenged for defending the targeting of civilians, Cheney is being heralded as a politician with "principles" willing to stand by his "convictions."

What are these principles and convictions? The principle that civilians can be sacrificed without concern because the United States wanted a military solution to the Iraq/Kuwait crisis? The conviction to never reflect on one's complicity in war crimes?

Why are Democrats—eager to challenge Bush's "compassionate conservative" label—not going after Cheney's war record? Why would opponents sink their teeth into every questionable business deal or nasty vote but steer clear of his Pentagon record?

Perhaps because the Gulf War remains popular with much of the U.S. public, but also because on these matters, there is little difference between Republicans and Democrats.

It appears that the discussion of Iraq in the upcoming campaign will not be about the moral imperative of lifting the sanctions and dealing with the widespread malnutrition, water-borne diseases and social disintegration in Iraq. Instead, the only question is whether the Clinton administration has been tough enough on Saddam Hussein. George W. Bush hints that if elected, he'll take more serious steps to oust Hussein. Clinton administration officials defend their starve-and-bomb strategy (in addition to the sanctions, the United States continues the regular, and quite illegal, bombing of Iraq in the so-called "no-fly zones").

Neither party wants to face the ugly reality that the 1991 war and the policies that have followed—in Republican and Democratic administrations—have killed innocents by the hundreds of thousands. They have not promoted democracy in Iraq, improved the lot of the Iraqi people, nor made the region any safer.

Those policies have failed the people who live in the region, but they have been effective—at least in the short term—in helping impose U.S. dominance in the Middle East. That is the principle underlying the Gulf War and the ongoing sanctions, and the conviction that keeps the sanctions in place.

Iraqis live under a brutal regime that protects its own interests ahead of its people, a regime with no conscience. When both major U.S. political parties agree that the suffering of innocents must continue, we must ask, "Where is the conscience of our nation?"

Clearly, not in Cheney, nor in any of the other candidates. The question is, can the consciences of ordinary Americans be stirred in time to help ordinary Iraqis?

Missile Defense

After a couple of embarrassing failures in previous tests and allegations that the military and contractors had tried to cover up the failures, the national missile defense (NMD) project was getting scrutiny from fairly mainstream sources. So, the test attracted attention in the news media. But most of the coverage of the planned test of a NMD system in the summer of 2000 focused on the technology. Left undiscussed, for the most part, was the question of why anyone would want such a system in the first place. That was a made-to-order situation for a radical op/ed.

I used the news peg of the missile test to make the obvious point that all these high-tech weapons systems—whether they work or not, whether they are needed or not—have always had one main purpose: to enrich the military contractors. I submitted the piece several weeks before the test to give editors as much flexibility in publishing it as possible.

I wrote this op/ed with *Newsday* in mind. Several months before this, a friend had published a piece in that paper and had given me the name of an editor there. I developed a relationship over email with the editor, and eventually he took this piece. I asked him about *Newsday*'s policy on submitting the piece to other papers, and he said that he wouldn't mind if I sent it to editors in Texas (not all that many Texas residents read the paper of Long Island). I did that, and the op/ed ended up running in the Dallas paper before it appeared in *Newsday*.

Missile shield's goal: Saving profits
Newsday, July 7, 2000, p. A-45;
Dallas Morning News, June 23, 2000, p. 25-A

When the U.S. missile defense system is tested today over the Pacific, much attention will be focused on whether the technology to shoot down nuclear warheads from much-feared "rogue states" is more than a pipe dream. But the focus on that question misses the program's main function.

The National Missile Defense (NMD) program—what began under President Ronald Reagan as the Strategic Defense Initiative (dubbed "Star Wars" by critics)—has shown it's capable of carrying out its primary mission, and the proof is in the numbers, not the performance tests.

Since Reagan first mentioned the idea in 1983, we have spent about $70 billion on missile-defense research. With both major-party presidential candidates supporting the project and pork-hungry representatives in Congress happy to vote more money, it's likely that billions more will be spent.

In short, the program does what it was designed to do: transfer money from the pockets of taxpayers to corporations.

Forget about the fact that the technical tests of the system have been failures, and that most everyone agrees a viable system is not within reach with technology we have or can reasonably imagine.

Forget that the timetable proposed would require huge financial commitments before anyone knows whether a system could ever work.

Forget about the fact that there exists no viable threat from which we must be protected. Forget that most of our allies, not to mention the rest of the world, seriously object to the concept and see it as a threat to world peace.

What matters to decision-makers is the flow of public subsidies for high-tech industries, always one of the key functions of the Pentagon budget.

The real targets of the NMD system are not the illusory incoming missiles, but the main missile contractors who will profit—Lockheed Martin, Boeing, Raytheon and TRW.

The companies "are looking to missile defense to revive them from mismanagement and technical problems that have slashed their stock prices and reduced their profit margins," according to the World Policy Institute's William Hartung, an observer of the weapons scene.

Hartung reports that these corporations have given $2 million to the 25 hard-core NMD boosters in the Senate and spent $34 million on lobbying during 1997-98. Interesting how the "national interest" tends to run so closely to corporate interests, and how the construction of threats to "national security" helps it run smoothly.

NMD helps with a serious problem for the military-industrial complex. With the demise of the Soviet Union, government, military and corporate officials faced a problem—how to justify huge expenditures on high-tech weapons systems with no evil empire to scare people.

Enter the rogue state. Now the gravest threat to our security is not a superpower, but countries such as Iraq, Iran and North Korea. Never mind that North Korea is on the brink of collapse and has begun conciliatory talks with South Korea, that Iran is acknowledged to be decades away from a workable long-range missile, or that a decade of cruel sanctions have crippled Iraq.

And never mind that every nation in the world knows that to launch a missile attack against the United States would be suicide, given the American willingness to use grotesque levels of violence to vanquish enemies.

As 1990s planners searched for ways to continue subsidies to high-tech industries, they found that Reagan's loopy SDI concept had legs. Many people had written off SDI as the product of Reagan's good-natured buffoonery, his penchant for Buck Rogers fantasies.

But when a no-nonsense policy wonk such as Al Gore endorses the concept, it's difficult to avoid the obvious truth—the system has nothing to do with defending the nation from missile attacks and everything to do with defending corporations from the harsh realities of the market.

This weapons con game has been going on since the end of World War II. If all it did was create dangerous (or useless) weapons, that would be bad enough.

But while we dump billions into such plans year after year, remember what is going underfunded or unfunded: quality education for all students, child care, national health insurance and a host of other social programs that could actually benefit the people of this country and serve the real national interest.

In an attempt to quiet objections around the world, President Bill Clinton has said the United States will share the NMD technology with "civilized nations." The only question is, what civilized nation would want it?

———————

Chapter 5

They've Got It All Wrong

It takes confidence (or hubris? arrogance?) to say, in effect, that virtually everyone talking about an issue in the mainstream is wrong. But that is what these op/eds do. In some cases, moderating a bit can be a good strategy to get a piece published, but these pieces work because they confront the conventional wisdom head on, arguing that the taken-as-obvious points are not only wrong but based on untenable assumptions—wrong all the way down, so to speak. The implication is that if people take the conventional view, they are either corrupt or not very bright (or both). In these kinds of pieces, the more one heightens the tension and challenges people to think the unthinkable, generally the more successful the piece.

These pieces play off some question in the news, though not necessarily a pressing and timely news event. If editors are intrigued enough by the attempt to turn conventional wisdom on its head, they won't care if the news hook is not immediate. The appeal of the pieces is in the haughty premise.

Terrorism

One of the most important realities to convey to Americans is that the United States government is a principal threat to, not the ultimate guarantor of, world peace. Piercing the rhetoric of America-as-the-force-for-peace is crucial if radical movements are going to make headway in stopping U.S. aggression abroad.

So, whenever I read about terrorist acts and rogue states, I look for ways to craft an op/ed that challenges the ways those terms are used in the mainstream. The 1998 U.S. missile attacks on Afghanistan and Sudan, allegedly to target terrorist forces responsible for the bombings of U.S. embassies in Kenya and Tanzania, offered such an opportunity as the mainstream news media ignored the obvious fact that the United States was the rogue.

Eventually journalists wrote about the fact that the alleged chemical plant in the Sudan was actually a pharmaceutical plant, and that the United States had severely crippled that country's drug-production system. But even then, mainstream journalists ignored the issue of international law and U.S. aggression.

The United States, a terrorist nation
Austin American-Statesman, September 1, 1998, p. A-9

U.S. officials and terrorism "experts" are filling the airwaves with talk of the threat that terrorism poses in the coming century. They have part of it right—terrorism will remain a threat. What they forget, ignore or deny is that the biggest perpetrator of terrorism on the world scene is the United States.

The United States, a terrorist nation?

That may seem like an odd statement to many, maybe even lunatic. It may seem treasonous, perhaps even blasphemous. But it is, unfortunately, one of those painfully obvious truths that, as a nation, we rarely allow ourselves to understand. And, just as obvious, is the fact that we will continue to suffer the terrorist attacks of others until we come to terms with this.

There is no one widely accepted definition of terrorism, though I suspect many would agree that the core of the concept involves the intentional killing of civilians or military personnel to effect political change, outside the widely accepted conventions of warfare and international law.

In reality, the term is used in the United States with a footnote: Terrorism is that kind of killing, unless it is the United States pulling the trigger.

So, the bombings of our embassies in Kenya and Tanzania are quite rightly labeled terrorist attacks and, quite rightly, condemned. But our retaliatory attacks on a base in Afghanistan and a factory in Sudan are widely viewed here as heroic acts. Yet in legal terms, both sets of attacks are clearly outside international law.

No matter how much administration officials obfuscate that reality, the U.S. cruise missile attacks were illegal under the UN charter, which allows for military action only in self-defense against an armed attack before the Security Council has a chance to act. The United States didn't even go through the motions of seeking Security Council action, as the charter requires in cases such as this. The administration's claim that this act of "self-defense" conforms to the UN charter is laughable, though widely accepted.

This is nothing new in U.S. history, especially in the post-World War II era. When the UN and international law are useful in pursuing policy, we are happy to use them. When they become annoyances that stand in the way of policy, we ignore them.

In its attack on South Vietnam, the United States bombed civilians, drenched the country in chemicals to destroy crops, and engaged in terrorist counterinsurgency campaigns to eliminate political opposition. Three different administrations engaged in these blatant violations of international law.

When the World Court handed down a judgment in 1986 that the United States had violated international law in its support of the contra's terrorist attack on Nicaragua, the Reagan administration simply refused to acknowledge the court's jurisdiction.

When the Bush administration planned the illegal invasion of Panama to arrest its dictator (and former CIA employee) Manuel Noriega in 1989, they felt the need to call it "Operation Just Cause" in a vain attempt to hide the obvious. Two years later in the Gulf War, the Bush administration pushed the violations of international law to even more murderous levels with the indiscriminate bombing of civilian areas, willful destruction of civilian infrastructure, and killing of retreating soldiers in Iraq.

The Clinton administration, first with its illegal missile attack on Iraq in 1993 and now with the most recent strikes, is the most recent U.S. regime to join this hall of shame.

The list could go on and on, covering U.S. overt and covert actions in Latin America, Southeast Asia, and the Middle East. And that's before we get to the actions of client regimes and private terror armies that have been backed by the United States.

In the debate this past summer over the configuration of an international criminal court, the United States repeatedly defended its opposition to a strong court by saying it did not want its military personnel hauled in front of such a court on "frivolous charges." The victims of past U.S. terrorism can easily attest to the fact that our sins are hardly frivolous.

None of these remarks, of course, should be taken as support of or rationalizations for terrorist acts committed by other nations or individuals. Nor is it an attack on the front-line military personnel who fought in these conflicts. I want only to suggest that if our actions in the world are to have any moral force, consistent application of international law to our own actions is a minimal requirement.

Palestinians and Peace

It's difficult to think of an issue on which the mainstream news media are more in lockstep with the position of the U.S. government than on Israel/Palestine. Even those who might be sympathetic to the Palestinian cause usually swallow without question the notion that the "peace process" laid out in the Oslo accords was aimed at a genuine peace. That sellout of the Palestinian people was made possible in the aftermath of the Gulf War, when U.S. power in the Middle East was beyond challenge and the international community allowed the Americans and Israelis to solidify the subordination of the Palestinians. One of the key aims for those interested in peace *and justice* in that region has to be a challenge to the very terms used. Even if the so-called peace process is implemented without substantive change, it's important to help people understand what has happened.

This piece illustrates how grassroots feedback to a newspaper can have an effect. A conversation with a national activist on the Palestine question led to a brief exchange with an activist in St. Louis, who was trying to get the paper there to run pieces critical of U.S. and Israeli policy. I sent the editor one op/ed that didn't run, but this second try a few months later was successful. That is a reminder that even a piece that doesn't end up in the paper isn't wasted; it can be the foundation for publication of a subsequent op/ed.

A peace process to break the hearts of Palestinians
St. Louis Post-Dispatch, September 27, 1999, p. D-17

As the Israeli government and the "Palestinian Authority" lumber ahead in final status talks that began this month, U.S. officials and the mainstream media continue to present this as one more important breakthrough on the way to concluding the "peace process" that might end in the declaration of a "Palestinian state."

But all that is breaking are the hearts of the Palestinian people and anyone else who once dreamed of real peace and real justice in the Middle East. Clarifying the terms in quotation marks can help us understand these broken dreams.

Peace process—The Oslo accords signed in 1993 instituted not a peace process but a capitulation process, the abandonment of the legitimate aspirations of the Palestinian people to regain the land from which they were expelled beginning in 1948. In the name of this peace process, Palestinian elites now scurry for any scraps that the Israelis might throw their way.

The Wye agreements signed in 1998 changed nothing, reinforcing an Israeli policy designed to secure the best land and retain control of the water resources of the West Bank and Gaza Strip while terminating responsibility for the Palestinian population. With settlements on the ground and the demolition of Palestinian homes and confiscation of Palestinian land continuing, Israel can maintain some features of the occupation while ridding itself of obligations to the occupied peoples, which have been turned over to the Palestinian Authority.

As the Israelis and Palestinian Authority have quibbled over what percentage of the West Bank should be transferred to full or partial Authority control or when a Palestinian state might be declared, it has been easy to overlook the fact that Israel is an occupying power in violation of international law in all of the West Bank. A basic principle of international law is that lands taken by force must be returned, and UN Security Council Resolution 242 calls for the withdrawal of Israel from territories taken in the 1967 war, including the West Bank and Gaza.

Although Oslo rendered 242 effectively dead, and some future agreement might bury 242 legally, the moral imperatives have not changed: Israeli aggression and flaunting of international law have paid off handsomely, and Israel should be held accountable.

If this is peace, it is not clear how much more peace the Palestinians can survive.

Palestinian Authority—The irony of the name is that while the Palestinian Authority is authoritarian in nature, it has precious little autonomous authority. While it has a huge police force, it is so tied to Israel that independent action is almost impossible. To keep negotiations going, the Authority has had to agree to become the enforcer for Israeli "security concerns," which has meant that its own instincts toward authoritarian control have only been intensified.

The Israeli demand for a policy of "zero tolerance" of terrorism from the Palestinian Authority means unjustified arrest campaigns, unlawful detention, excessive force and arbitrary restrictions on free expression. Much like in the Bantustan governments created by South Africa under apartheid to give the appearance of black self-rule, the Palestinian Authority has the right to police its people and administer a system designed to keep them powerless and in poverty.

If this is authority for Palestinians, it's little more than the authority to preside over one's own second-class status.

Palestinian state—At this point, many Israelis have no problem accepting a Palestinian state, given that such a state will be poor, militarily powerless, and cut into pieces by Israeli settlements and roads. The division of resources and distribution of real power in the region won't be altered by the declaration of a Palestinian state.

Some fanatics still hold on to the notion that no Palestinian state can ever be accepted, but increasingly they are on the fringe. Even before his election as prime minister, Ehud Barak was calling a Palestinian state a "de facto phenomenon." He explained, "We don't have to intervene with their decisions about stamps and passports."

Barak has nothing to fear from a Palestinian state that has few resources and is subordinated to Israel in security matters. It will be a state in technical terms—issuing stamps and passports—but little else.

If this is a state, then being stateless has attractive features.

As always, these matters should be of serious concern to U.S. citizens, given that U.S. diplomatic support and financial and military aid have long allowed Israel to pursue these policies. The relationship between the two countries has not been without friction as strategic interests have sometimes diverged, but in the end it is not only Israeli but U.S. policy that has broken the hearts of the Palestinian people.

Gulf War

Of all my short op/ed pieces, this challenge to the conventional wisdom about the Gulf War sparked the most outraged mail. I heard from active duty military personnel, folks who had served in the war, and other citizens—most of whom told me I was a despicable person and a sad excuse for an American for criticizing the military.

The response didn't surprise me; it's been my experience that holding the U.S. military and politicians accountable for war crimes is a sure way to anger Americans. It was especially threatening to suggest that the war that was supposed to have helped Americans regain their national pride was in fact a depraved exercise in mass murder.

It is worth pointing out that it's unlikely that any paper would have published this kind of piece during or immediately after the Gulf War. What little critique of this kind there is in the mainstream usually is allowed only when the events are safely in the past. But that doesn't mean that writing about it in retrospect is not useful politically; for many of us, being forced to rethink past American "adventures" that we thought were noble has been a crucial experience in turning radical. In the case of Iraq, the ongoing war against the people of Iraq through routine bombings and an economic embargo make this exercise in history even more relevant.

The Gulf War brought out the worst in us
Los Angeles Times, May 22, 2000, p. B-7

Did a U.S. general in the Gulf War violate rules of engagement and, in effect, murder Iraqis after the cease-fire?

That's the claim of journalist Seymour Hersh in the May 22 *New Yorker* magazine. The former general and current federal drug czar, Barry McCaffrey, has counter-punched, arguing that he is the victim of a journalistic vendetta.

Which one is right? It doesn't really matter.

The incidents Hersh writes about are, in the context of the massacre we call the Gulf War, relatively trivial, and therein lies the problem with the controversy. By focusing on the actions of a commander in a limited arena, we risk forgetting what U.S. military forces did in Iraq in 1991—across the board, on a daily basis, in full view of all the world, with impunity. What we did has a name in the rest of the world, though it can't be spoken in polite circles here: war crimes.

We have yet to come to terms with the enormity of the crimes our government and military carried out in 1991. If Hersh's allegations are true, McCaffrey's conduct was reprehensible and criminal, but those actions pale in comparison with the brutality the U.S. military unleashed on the people of Iraq throughout the war.

What brutality? What crimes? Start with the most basic facts about the U.S. attack on civilians and civilian infrastructure in Iraq.

The Geneva Conventions are clear on these matters: "Civilians shall not be the object of attack." The charge to military forces in the UN Security Council resolution was to expel the Iraqi forces that had invaded Kuwait. To do that, we dropped 88,000 tons of bombs over Iraq, one of the most concentrated attacks on an entire society in modern warfare. Those bombs killed civilians—both directly and over time through the destruction of the country's power grid, food, water treatment and sewage systems. Some of that bombing of civilians was targeted, some indiscriminate; both are war crimes under the Geneva Conventions.

Recall the "Highway of Death," the deadly stretch of road in Kuwait that was littered with burned-out vehicles and charred bodies. U.S. military forces, in violation of international law, fired on retreating and largely defenseless Iraqi soldiers just before the cease-fire. U.S. pilots described it in news accounts as a "turkey shoot" and "like shooting fish in a barrel." The carnage was not only unnecessary but grotesque.

Remember the brutality of U.S. weapons. We used napalm to incinerate entrenched Iraqi soldiers. We dropped fuel-air explosives, ghastly weapons often called "near-nukes" because of their destructive capacity through fire, asphyxiation and concussion. We dropped cluster bombs that use razor-sharp fragments to shred people. To penetrate tanks, we used depleted-uranium shells, the long-term health effects of which are unknown. Widely accepted notions of proportionality and protection of civilians go out the window with such weapons.

Although the shooting war has stopped, the most onerous economic embargo ever imposed on a nation continues today. Supposedly designed to rein in the regime of Saddam Hussein, the harsh economic sanctions have only killed innocents—as many as 1 million in the past decade, according to UN studies.

In short: It is misleading to call the Gulf War a war; it was a massacre. In the words of British journalist Geoff Simons, who has studied the war in detail, it was "a massive slaughter of a largely helpless enemy, with much of the killing occurring after the time when constructive diplomacy would have brought an end to the conflict and a secure liberation of Kuwait."

That is an assessment many people—likely the vast majority—around the world would agree with, but one rarely voiced in this country.

My goal is not to defend McCaffrey. But no matter how guilty he might be, I fear that demonizing him will divert us from assessing the responsibility of those politicians and top officers who planned and executed the slaughter. And it will keep us from asking why we—citizens with so much political freedom—have done so little to hold those politicians and officers accountable for the crimes committed in our name.

———

Vietnam Apologies

This is one of two op/eds about Vietnam included in this book. They were written within six months of each other and share the common theme that the United States still cannot tell itself basic truths about our attack on Vietnam. The first piece was tied to the anniversary of the end of the war, while this one plays off President Clinton's visit.

Attentive readers will notice that a couple of paragraphs are identical. The next time I see a new hook for another Vietnam piece, I will write. I will continue to do so as long as the history of that war is so distorted in the textbooks and in the public imagination. I will continue to fine-tune the argument, searching for better ways to present the case, but I won't hesitate to reuse phrases or paragraphs that work. I may get bored with writing the same piece, but the same piece needs to be written as often as possible.

One of the reasons mainstream media have such a powerful influence over what we think is that certain core ideas are repeated over and over, a drumbeat of conventional wisdom. Radicals will never have the resources or channels to match that, but we can be diligent in always looking for openings to assert a different view of history.

Even now, we lie to ourselves about Vietnam
Austin American-Statesman, November 25, 2000, p. A-15

Bill Clinton has always been keen on apologizing, for himself and on behalf of the nation. He has apologized not only for a sex scandal, but for U.S. support of repression in Guatemala and slavery.

One might contest the motivation for, or the phrasing of, the apologies—Were they offered for the right reason? Did they go far enough?—but at least they were offered.

There is one act of contrition, however, that Clinton—or any American leader—has not been able to make.

On his way to Hanoi last week, when asked if he thought the United States owed the people of Vietnam an apology, 25 years after the end of the war, Clinton said, simply, "No, I don't."

Some have offered a personalized explanation. As a man who avoided the draft during that war, Clinton has to stand tough today. But another possibility deserves consideration: To apologize for crimes against the people of Vietnam would be to admit that the stories we tell ourselves about our conduct in the world — then and now — are a lie.

To apologize would be to acknowledge that while we claimed to be defending democracy, we were derailing democracy. While we claimed to be defending South Vietnam, we were attacking the people of South Vietnam.

To apologize now would be to admit that the rationalizations for post-World War II U.S. foreign policy have been, and are still today, rhetorical cover for the power politics of an empire.

The standard story in the United States about that war is that in our quest to guarantee peace and freedom for Vietnam, we misunderstood its history, politics and culture, leading to mistakes that doomed our effort. Some argue we should have gotten out sooner than we did; others suggest we should have fought harder. But the common ground in mainstream opinion is that our motives were noble.

But we never fought in Vietnam for democracy. After World War II, the United States supported and financed France's attempt to retake its former colony. After the Vietnamese defeated the French in 1954, the Geneva Conference called for free elections in 1956, which the United States and its South Vietnamese client regime blocked. In his memoirs, President Eisenhower explained why: In free elections, the communists would have won by an overwhelming margin. The United States is all for elections, as long as they turn out the way we want.

The central goal of U.S. policymakers in Vietnam had nothing to do with freedom for the Vietnamese people, but instead was to make sure that an independent socialist course of development did not succeed. U.S. leaders invoked Cold War rhetoric about the threat of the communist monolith but really feared that a "virus" of independent development might infect the rest of Asia, perhaps even becoming a model for all the Third World.

To prevent the spread of the virus, we dropped 6.5 million tons of bombs and 400,000 tons of napalm on the people of Southeast Asia. Saturation bombing of civilian areas, counterterrorism programs and political assassination, routine killings of civilians and 11.2 million gallons of Agent Orange to destroy crops and ground cover—all were part of the U.S. terror war in Vietnam, as well as Laos and Cambodia.

This interpretation is taken as obvious in much of the world, yet it is virtually unspeakable in polite and respectable circles in this country, which says much about the moral quality of polite and respectable people here.

Why is the truth about our attack on Vietnam so difficult to acknowledge? I think it is not just about Vietnam but about a larger truth concerning our role in the world. We are the empire. Especially in the past half-century, we have supported repressive regimes around the world as long as they served elite interests. We have violated international law in countless invasions and interventions. While talking about the inviolate nature of human rights, we have trampled those rights and the legitimate aspirations of liberation movements.

In many ways, the Vietnam War was the defining act of the United States as empire, an aggression that was condemned around the world and at home, but pursued nonetheless, as the body count went into the millions. It is the linchpin of our mythology about ourselves.

In his last years on Earth, Martin Luther King Jr. understood this, as he began to speak out forcefully against the war. "If America's soul becomes totally poisoned, part of the autopsy must read 'Vietnam,'" King said in 1967.

If he were alive today, I don't know whether King would give up on the soul of America and write a final autopsy report. But I am confident he would argue forcefully that the future is lost as long as we let stand the poisonous distortions of history.

Chapter 6

Piggybacking on the News

If news is what is new, then how does a writer find openings for timeless truths that are politically important? It's important for radical activists to keep the focus on systems and structures of power, and the ideology used to support them. That means finding a way to talk about the oppression inherent in a capitalist, patriarchal, and white-supremacist society.

It's difficult to write a general critique of, say, patriarchy and its institutions and practices that will be very attractive to a mainstream editor. There are times, however, when a news story can be used as a springboard for an op/ed that isn't directly concerned with the news item itself and allows that kind of deep critique. Because editors feel safer with a piece that plays off something current, it's always good to keep an eye open for that kind of opportunity.

Each of these op/eds was an attempt to use an event or comment by a public official to highlight just such a basic critique. The pieces may seem pretty transparent; in each case, I am clearly not interested in the news item that serves as the hook. But these remind us that the main thing an op/ed has to do is catch the fancy of an editor. I've had editors tell me that they don't like "thumbsucker" pieces that pontificate on "big ideas." That's generally the case. But if you use enough of a current news hook, it's possible to slip a few big ideas in.

God's Chosen?

I have long been incensed with Americans, especially politicians, claiming that the United States has a unique destiny in the world as the shining city on the hill. Sometimes the talk is secular, and sometimes God has a hand in it. Whatever the source of the special status, it is a ridiculous claim, but a key part of the rhetoric that keeps Americans believing that the leaders of the country can, at least in foreign affairs, do no wrong.

I have a file on my desk called "American BS" in which I throw references to this idea. I draw on that file for public talks, and for more than a year I was on the lookout for an opening to write an op/ed on the subject. That chance came when the then-governor of Texas George W. Bush threw out the "chosen by God" line in an attempt to cover his butt on racial issues. By this time, I was ready to pounce on the opportunity, having worked out a concise piece in my head over the past year or so. The fact that Bush is a Texas boy no doubt helped the piece make it into two of the state's biggest papers.

Idea that U.S. is God's chosen is dangerous
San Antonio Express-News, March 21, 2000, p. 7-B;
Dallas Morning News, March 24, 2000, p. 25-A

"For all my flaws, I believe I have been chosen by God and commissioned by history to be the model to the world of justice and inclusion and diversity without division."

If I dared utter such words in public, people rightly would laugh at the absurdity of the claim or angrily chastise me for my arrogance, or both. On the surface, the hubris of the statement suggests I am the person least likely to be chosen by God to do anything but embarrass myself.

Yet when George W. Bush—trying to recover from his association with the painfully public bigotry of Bob Jones University— boldly proclaimed last week that the United States had been so chosen and commissioned, it was dutifully reported in the press without a hint of irony or sarcasm.

Forget about the obvious problems with his statement as it applies to race and ethnicity—that those "flaws," which include a brutal history of genocide of indigenous people, African slavery and the legalized subordination of nonwhites, and an ongoing social and economic apartheid, render the claim absurd. The deeper problem with Bush's remarks is what we might call the pathology of the anointed.

The invocation of a direct connection to God and truth is a peculiar, and particularly dangerous, feature of American history. The story we tell ourselves goes something like this:

Other nations throughout history have acted out of greed and self-interest, seeking territory, wealth and power. They often did bad things in the world. Then came the United States, touched by God, a shining city on the hill, whose leaders created the first real democracy and went on to be the beacon of freedom for people around the world. Unlike the rest of the world, we act out of a cause nobler than greed; we are both the model and the vehicle for bringing peace, freedom, and democracy to the world.

That is a story that can be believed only in the United States — and there only by a certain privileged segment of the population — by people sufficiently insulated from the reality of U.S. actions abroad to maintain such illusions.

But try selling the idea to the people of Guatemala, still rebuilding their country from the legacy of four decades of terror at the hands of a military government installed and funded by the United States.

Try explaining the United States' chosen status to the children of Iraq, who are dying at the rate of 5,000 a month because this country continues to back the harshest economic embargo in modern history.

Try defending the thesis to the people of Vietnam, who for a decade stood up to U.S. bombs, bullets and chemical warfare because they wouldn't accept "freedom" managed by a U.S. puppet government.

The United States, in short, acts like a nation-state, and nation-states are not benevolent institutions. For much of its history, the United States also has been a great power, and the record of great powers is even less savory. Now, as what folks like to call "the lone superpower," the future behavior of U.S. policymakers is unlikely to suddenly become saintly.

We expect individuals who proclaim themselves chosen by God or commissioned by history either to be hucksters, cloaking themselves in a higher calling to cover crasser motives, or simply psychotic. There is no reason to think anything else when such claims are made at the level of the nation-state.

It is tempting to laugh at and dismiss these rhetorical flour-
ishes of pandering politicians, but the commonness of the chosen-
by-God assertions and the lack of outrage or amusement at them
suggests that the claims are taken seriously by both significant
segments of the public and the politicians. Just as it has been in
the past, the consequences of this pathology of the anointed will
be borne not by those chosen by God, but by those against whom
God's-chosen decide to take aim.

Corporate Capitalism

After the WTO meeting in Seattle was over, I knew there was a
window for post-protest analysis. I also knew that the wire services would be full of syndicated columns doing just that. Rather
than offer my take on what had happened, I used the opening to
hit on the bigger issue of corporate power, which has to be central
to any serious radical critique at this point in history.

So, the piece mentions the WTO, but only enough to provide a
hook. It's not really a piece about the WTO or the protests, and the
editors who accepted the piece could see this, of course. But because the question of corporate power was in the air, it was a
piece that made sense to them. I'm sure that if I had written essen-
tially the same piece with no news hook, it would have been far
more difficult—indeed, perhaps impossible—to get in the paper.

I was glad to see a piece this directly aimed at capitalism in the
paper for its own sake, but I think it also had a larger positive
effect. The op/ed resulted in a larger-than-usual response to me
directly, and based on the letters to the editor that were published,
readers took notice of it and let the paper know what they
thought. Not all were supportive, of course, but that's not crucial.
When editors get feedback that tells them radical writing gets
readers' attention, it makes them more likely to run more of such
work.

Corporate power is the central issue
Austin American-Statesman, December 10, 1999, p. A15

Anyone who followed the protests of the World Trade Organiza-tion meeting in Seattle can likely name the chain coffee house that had its windows broken (Starbucks), the color of the clothing worn by the demonstrators who broke the windows (the "black-clad" anarchists), or the cartoon characters the riot-gear-clad Seattle police most resembled (Ninja Turtles).

But how many know what brought the protesters into the streets? The demonstrations were the result of a coalition of labor, environmental and human-rights groups, each bringing their own specific concerns. But we were told little about those concerns, and even less about the simple principle that brings those groups together:

Corporations shouldn't run the world, people should.

The central question for the global economy is not free trade v. protectionism. It's whether we will have trade rules designed to benefit corporations or people. Does "economic growth" mean only an increase in corporate profits, or does it mean a decent life for people?

The corporate propagandists, and their supporters in the Clin-ton administration, would like us to believe that what benefits the corporations by definition benefits people—the "a rising tide lifts all boats" argument.

When rising corporate profits coincide with stagnating real wages for the majority of Americans and continued sweatshop conditions in the developing world, that's an increasingly hard line to sell. Slowly, people are coming to understand a few obvi-ous truths about the corporate entities that control much of our lives: Corporations are authoritarian institutions that are incom-patible with democracy.

That simple assertion is at odds, of course, with the current rhetoric, which tells us that "free markets" open to huge transna-tional corporations are the defining feature of democracy. There is no greater testament to the power of modern public relations and advertising than the fact that such a patently absurd claim is taken so seriously.

First, there is no such thing as a free market, if free means "open to all with equality of opportunity." As many in the developing world point out, it is quite convenient for the industrial nations of the world—which built their economies on some combination of protectionism, slavery and imperial conquest—now to proselytize for free markets. In such a setting, free markets mean nothing more than the freedom of transnational corporations to exploit more freely the people and resources of the less-developed nations.

And what of modern corporations? On what principles are they built?

As anyone who has ever worked in one knows, there is no such thing as democracy within a corporation. By law and tradition, authority is vested in the hands of a small number of directors who empower managers to wield control. Those managers on occasion might solicit the views of workers below; it is usually called "seeking input." But input does not translate into the power to effect change and implement policy.

Corporations exist for one reason only—to maximize profit. Neither history nor logic give us any reason to think that maximizing profit leads to democracy within a corporation or support for democracy in the society. U.S. corporations, which do their best to subvert meaningful democracy at home through bribes to politicians commonly called campaign contributions, have shown repeatedly that when given a choice in other countries, they prefer dictatorships and oligarchies to real democracies. Rule by iron-fisted thugs and elites generally is easier to deal with than a government based on popular sovereignty.

So, the central problem of the WTO is that it was designed by and for corporations, not people. Its rules are made and enforced in secrecy, with no pretense of democracy. And those rules subvert the democratic processes that exist in some nations.

Some protesters want the WTO reformed. I lean toward scrapping it; the people of the world have a better shot at protecting themselves from corporate predators without such an organization around to protect the wealthy. But whatever the position taken on the WTO, the focus has to remain on the central task:

Unless we, the sovereign people, revise our laws to reign in, and eventually dismantle, the modern corporation, we will always be fighting battles in which we are outgunned and outspent.

We cannot have a meaningful democracy at home, or promote democracy abroad, if we live most of our lives under the thumbs of authoritarian institutions that concentrate wealth and power in the hands of the few to the detriment of the many.

If that sounds like old-fashioned rhetoric, it is. Working people understood it at the turn of the last century as they fought a losing battle against the emergence of corporate power. As this century turns, the battle continues, now with fresh spirit. This time, we can't afford to lose.

Sexual Harassment

The national obsession with the Clinton impeachment story was annoying to me on two counts. First, I supported impeaching Clinton, but for his war crimes in Iraq, Afghanistan, and Sudan (his crimes in Yugoslavia were yet to come at this point), not for his sexual behavior. Second, I found it absurd for people to pretend that his abuse of power in the sexual arena was somehow unusual. So, I wasn't really concerned about Clinton, but I knew that the easiest way to make the point about the nature of a patriarchal sexual system was to hang the piece on the president.

I rarely publish op/eds in the campus newspaper, mainly because it is a student forum that I think should be reserved for students except in special circumstances. But in this case, I wanted to make sure as many professors as possible read the piece. In many arenas of life, such as physician-patient relations, it is well understood that a person (almost always a man) in a position of authority or trust should not engage in sexual or romantic behavior with the person in a vulnerable position. But one can find a significant number of professors who will argue that sexual relationships between students and teachers are acceptable, unless the student is in a class with the professor at the time.

Although some might see a campus paper as a lesser vehicle for an op/ed, my experience suggests that college papers are read closely by a higher percentage of university students, staff, and faculty than the local daily is read closely by residents. The lively letters-to-the-editor sections in college papers are testimony to the interest in those papers, especially in their op/ed pages.

As is often the case these days, this piece subsequently was posted on the Internet by *feminista*, an online feminist journal.

Clinton: A common male practice
Daily Texan, September 17, 1998, p. 4

The way to understand what's important about the Bill Clinton scandal is to quit obsessing about what this means about Bill Clinton and pay attention to what it means about our society. With all this talk about sin, we forget to think about the systems and structures, about how power made what Bill Clinton did commonplace.

So, let's look at the facts.

A middle-aged man with a lot of power in an organization decides to get sexual gratification from a much younger woman who works for him. In short, what Bill Clinton did was normal.

By normal, I don't mean good. I don't mean his behavior should set the norms for others. By normal, I mean that it happens a lot, and it happens for a perfectly predictable reason: The behavior is in line with the norms of our society.

Now, by norms, I don't mean what we say we believe as a society, but instead the actual rules that govern our lives. I'm referring not to rhetoric, but reality.

We live in a world structured by, among other things, male dominance. In our world, male dominance is expressed through, among other things, sex. Sex becomes one way in which male power is made real. In such a society, sex becomes most sexy when it is an expression of power and dominance. And in a society in which men hold the vast majority of positions of power, the results are not difficult to predict.

What Bill Clinton and Monica Lewinsky did was, by all accounts, consensual. Clinton's actions appear not to rise to the level of sexual harassment, in a legal sense. Apparently, he did not create a hostile climate, nor did he use a quid pro quo demand to get sex.

But simply because Clinton did nothing illegal does not mean his actions were not an abuse of power. I'm not talking in Ken Starr terms here. I am talking about the routine abuse of power that countless politicians, business executives, professors, and ministers commit when they poach on younger women who are subordinate to them in an organization.

In my own world, higher education, such abuse goes on daily. Faculty members, almost exclusively male, use their power and position to sleep with students. Every professor I know can cite at least several examples, and I wouldn't have to walk very far in my own building to bump into a male colleague who has had sex with a student.

The common response to this kind of critique is that when the women consent to, or perhaps even initiate, such relationships, how can we call it an abuse of power? Is it not an insult to a woman to suggest she is a dupe of patriarchy? Can't women choose for themselves?

Of course they can. I have no doubt that women engage in such relationships for a variety of reasons. Some may love the man they become involved with. Others may do it to gain some advantage in the organization. Some may do it because they feel flattered, others because they're afraid to say no.

But it is not insulting to anyone to acknowledge how systems of power structure the world in which we live. We all make choices under varying levels of constraints and freedom. My point is that in trying to understand and resist those unjust systems of power, we should focus on the actions of those with the most power not the least, because it is the powerful who should be most accountable.

So, asking why the woman does it is the wrong question. The more important question is, why does the man do it? What is it about our society's definitions of masculinity, power and sex that lead to such routine abuse of women? Why do men poach on younger women? Why do men use pornography and prostitutes?

Why do men rape and beat and sexually harass women? Why is male sexuality so fused with self-indulgence, conquest and domination? And, most importantly, how do we change it?

It is the choices that men make that I am most concerned about. As a man, it is my actions that should be scrutinized the most closely. In any system of power, it is the decisions of those on top, of those who abuse their power, that should be our focus.

Bill Clinton, and every other man who abuses power in this way, should be held accountable. But the current hand-wringing over Clinton's behavior, as if he were the only man in this position, blocks us from learning from the scandal. Whether or not he is impeached is, to me, a rather trivial matter. More important is whether we learn anything from it about ourselves.

Chapter 7

Anniversaries and Holidays

One of the easiest news hooks for an op/ed is an anniversary. The culture in general seems to like the opportunity to look back, and journalists especially find them irresistible. I've always assumed that's because the obsession with what is new so often prevents reflection upon the past; so, journalists seize on anniversaries as one of their few openings for looking back.

Anniversaries are useful to all op/ed writers because they are predictable. One can look at the calendar and know that a piece on the tenth anniversary of an event could run on a specific date, allowing the luxury of planning. Instead of having to react quickly to the news, anniversary pieces offer a more leisurely pace for thinking and writing.

For radical writers, anniversaries offer a place for reinterpreting the standard explanation for an event or policy. For example, once the country's mistakes are safely in the past, the culture can sometimes acknowledge them. Because anniversaries fit into an existing story form, more radical analysis is often easier to slip in. And, as always, one should look for ways to connect past events to ongoing oppression in the contemporary world, teasing out the lessons in history that should be applied today.

El Salvador

In a piece on the tenth anniversary of the murder of the Jesuit intellectuals, contemporary connections were central. This piece comes close to violating the rule about not introducing too many ideas in one op/ed, which is why it is a bit longer than average. I tried to squeeze into it enough history of the civil war in El Salvador to give readers a sense of why the United States was culpable in the murders, and then went on to suggest that the United States was capable of such brutality in the present and at the same time had found other methods of control that seemed to be less brutal on the surface. Also thrown in are a few observations about moral obligation.

Probably the most important part of this op/ed is the challenge to Bill Clinton's apology about U.S. policy in Central America. Since U.S. politicians are so reluctant to ever admit mistakes, Clinton might be seen as admirable for the public declaration. But one constant task for radicals is to point out the emptiness of the rhetoric of the powerful and make it clear that real accountability has to include a genuine effort not to repeat the atrocities. Asking forgiveness is an empty gesture if there is no accompanying commitment to change.

El Salvador's sins a history lesson U.S. should heed
Houston Chronicle, November 15, 1999, p. 25-A

At dawn on Nov. 16, 1989, members of an elite Salvadoran military unit entered the campus of the University of Central America in San Salvador and murdered six Jesuit priests, their housekeeper and her 15-year-old daughter—eight victims added to the at least 70,000 others killed in El Salvador's civil war of the 1980s, the vast majority at the hands of state security forces and death squads.

The 10th anniversary of this crime will no doubt be observed all over El Salvador, but it also should be highlighted in the United States, where government officials bear considerable responsibility for the murders, not only of those eight but of all those victims of the civil war. It was with U.S. funding and active U.S. support that the Salvadoran military and reactionary elements of that society carried out the atrocities. Simple moral decency demands that we understand our culpability.

This anniversary is more than just a history lesson; we should mark it also to remind us that the United States is continuing the same pattern in Colombia, where under the cover of the drug war we are arming a country with the worst human-rights record in the hemisphere in the 1990s.

Since its independence from Spain in 1821, El Salvador was ruled by a small oligarchy and a military noted for its brutal control of a poverty-stricken population. The harsh repression intensified in 1979, symbolized most notably by the murder of Archbishop Oscar Romero by the military in 1980.

The brutality of the state forces we were funding and training didn't bother U.S. policymakers. President Carter ignored Romero's pleas to stop the flow of weapons, and President Reagan increased funding, weapons, and training. The Atlacatl Battalion that carried out the murders of the Jesuits was formed in 1981 when U.S. counterinsurgency specialists were sent to El Salvador to train what would become a notoriously savage unit that could take credit for some of the country's worst massacres.

Rebel forces and the government signed a peace treaty in 1992, after the United States had funneled $6 billion over 12 years to the killers and tens of thousands of corpses had piled up. This year, with U.S.-backed atrocities safely in the past, President Clinton did acknowledge our role in such atrocities. But his heartfelt apology about the dark and painful period rings hollow, for two reasons:

First, it's easy to be contrite when in the new global order the United States can more easily subjugate the economies of such countries through the use of international financial agencies like the International Monetary Fund and World Bank, which help break down resistance to domination by foreign capital. Increasingly, the dictators and torturers on whom the United States has traditionally relied are not necessary. As the region has sunk back into much of the poverty and inequality that sparked the wars, free trade has been adequate to do that job.

Second, U.S. leaders would not hesitate to support such brutality again if it were deemed necessary, as in Colombia. The Clinton administration wants to increase military aid by $2 billion over the next three years, hoping to sell the policy by claiming that the violence is primarily drug-related. The guerillas fighting the government fund themselves in part by providing protection for cocaine producers, and the guerillas have been responsible for human-rights violations, though on a far smaller scale than the government. But their struggle is rooted not in the drug trade, but in opposition to control of the country by a small elite that sees nothing wrong with impoverishing everyone else.

The goal of the U.S.-funded counterinsurgency campaign in Colombia, just as it was in El Salvador and Guatemala, is to keep

power in the hands of the rightful rulers—those who play ball
with U.S. strategic interests and corporations. Amnesty International estimates that the government and its allied forces killed
more than 1,000 civilians in 1998, but U.S. leaders have shown
they do not care that government forces, and the paramilitaries
tied to the government, are responsible for the vast majority of
these political killings in Colombia.

Unless the American people demand a change, the United
States will continue to fund, supply, and train the killers, as it did
in El Salvador.

The Jesuit intellectuals murdered by our proxies would have
understood this simple moral choice. They would have exhorted
us not to mourn only their deaths, but the countless deaths of the
poor and invisible in these struggles. They also would argue that
we not only honor the dead, but fight for the living who are the
likely victims of the current repression.

If Bill Clinton truly is sorry for the atrocities committed by his
predecessors, he would not knowingly commit the same sins in
Colombia. It is clear that we cannot rely on his conscience, but on
our own. Let us allow the memory of the murdered Jesuits to
engage our conscience.

Rethinking Vietnam

This piece was a bit of a gamble. The argument I try to make in it
is not terribly complex, but it pushes the edge of what one can do
in a short space. I took a shot at it because the propaganda about
why and how we fought the Vietnam War is so pervasive that it
takes a serious assault on the conventional wisdom to get people
to consider an alternative explanation.

The other problem with the piece is that the lack of space prevented me from acknowledging that my simple assertions were
not so simple. While in some respects the United States clearly did
win the Vietnam War, there were other effects, at least in the
short-term, that gave strength to movements for liberation in
other parts of the world.

One concern that I didn't anticipate came from a journalist in the alternative press who told me that he was wary of taking a case in which dissidents had managed a sustained protest of U.S. policy that was in some ways successful, and then turning around and calling it a victory for the government. Will activists, or potential activists, who have always thought of that antiwar movement as one of the few successes be less likely to engage in politics in the future if they are told that movement failed? His challenge reminded me that there are a number of different considerations that must be kept in mind when writing for a mainstream audience. As one is trying to reach nonradical readers, it's important to remember that other radicals will be reading.

Vietnam War is a study in U.S. crimes
Detroit Free Press, April 28, 2000, p. 11-A

Twenty-five years ago today, the last helicopter took off from the roof of an apartment building near the U.S. embassy in Saigon—a powerful image of Americans getting out just before the Vietnamese we fought against took over the city from the Vietnamese we supported. The photo of that scene that ran in papers around the country remains a symbol of our defeat in the Vietnam War.

But there's a problem with that symbol and that memory: We won the Vietnam War.

U.S. policymakers have won a huge propaganda victory in shaping perceptions about that war and, paradoxically, one of the propaganda achievements has been convincing people that we lost. The reason for the seemingly strange strategy is simple. Putting forward the idea that we lost obscures both the real reason we fought the war and diverts attention from U.S. crimes during the war.

Despite the incessant claims of U.S. leaders, we did not fight in Vietnam to establish democracy. Instead, we fought in Vietnam to derail democracy. After the Vietnamese defeat of French colonialism in 1954, the Geneva Conference called for free elections in 1956. But the United States and its client regime in South Vietnam blocked those elections. Why? In his memoirs, President Eisenhower explained honestly: In free elections, the communists would have won by an overwhelming margin. As is typical, the United States is all for elections in other countries, if they turn out the way we want.

The central goal of U.S. policymakers in Vietnam was to make sure that an independent socialist course of development did not succeed. U.S. leaders relied on Cold War rhetoric about the communist monolith, but really feared that a "virus" of such independent development could infect the rest of Asia, perhaps even becoming a model for all the Third World. What might happen if all nations emerging from colonialism believed they had a right to decide their own futures, outside the U.S. orbit?

It is much easier to obscure these U.S. war aims if we talk about how we lost the war, leading to the fall of a South Vietnamese democracy that never existed. It also is easier to obscure the brutality of the U.S. war.

So long as we believe we lost the war, the question can be asked, "If we had fought harder, could we have won?" Some Americans still talk about how we fought the Vietnam War "with one hand tied behind our back," yet with only one hand, we managed to drop 6.5 million tons of bombs and 400,000 tons of napalm on the people of Southeast Asia. Short of nuclear weapons, it's not clear what kind of violence we could have unleashed on the people of Vietnam that we did not unleash.

If people can convince themselves that we were restrained gentlemen during the war, it is easier to ignore the saturation bombing of civilian areas, counterterrorism programs that included large-scale political assassination, routine killings of civilians, and 11.2 million gallons of Agent Orange to destroy crops and ground cover—all part of the U.S. terror war in not only Vietnam but Laos and Cambodia as well. All those are clear violations of international law—that is, war crimes.

Twenty-five years later, the virus U.S. policymakers feared has been largely stamped out, with only a few stubborn holdouts such as the Zapitistas in Chiapas. Southeast Asia—indeed, most of the Third World—is "safe" not only for U.S. style democracy (that is, democracy with results favorable to the United States) but for multinational corporations to take advantage of the resources and exploit the labor.

By telling the story that we lost the war, the United States can continue to evade the truth about its foreign policy. While it is true that we did not achieve total conquest of South Vietnam, 25 years later the nature of the U.S. victory is clear. Vietnam, still recovering from the massive destruction caused by the United States attack, is forced to accept—by economic pressure not bombs—its place in the international economic order run out of Washington and New York.

The Vietnamese people survived U.S. aggression as an independent people. The question is, will they survive their victory.

Cold War

As the tenth anniversary of the fall of the Berlin Wall approached, I received a message from a political organizer who was trying to use the anniversary to generate op/eds around the country that would argue for nuclear disarmament. I agreed to write it, but as I thought through the piece, I realized that arguing that the end of the Cold War meant we could now disarm would play into the notion that those nukes were ever necessary.

So, my direction for the piece changed. Instead of focusing on nuclear weapons, I decided to attack one of the most important propaganda victories of U.S. policymakers in my lifetime—the widespread acceptance of the conventional wisdom about the Cold War. So successful has that propaganda been that even most dissidents use the term in ways that concede the basic premise— that U.S. policy was motivated by fear of the Soviet threat to our very existence. I have many times found myself using the term, even when I know it needs to be taken apart, because it is so much a part of the language.

This is an example of the many difficult strategic decisions that must be made in radical politics. When is it better to play off some of the conventional wisdom to try to achieve a policy goal, and when is it better to go to the heart of the society's myths and challenge the delusions we hold about ourselves? As I have suggested, in op/ed writing as in all politics, there is usually no obvi-

ous answer to that question in any given situation, and certainly
no formula for answering that can be applied easily. It sometimes
reduces to a gut feeling, and in this case, my gut feeling was to
attack the deeper myth. I think the organizer who contacted me
leaned the other way, and it's clear that other op/eds in other cities
took the other tack. We can only hope that pluralism in strategies
helps us move forward.

---

10 years after the Berlin Wall fell,
it's time to junk the war machine
Austin American-Statesman, November 6, 1999, p. A-11

On Nov. 9, 1989, the Berlin Wall came tumbling down. A decade
later, it's time that one of the central myths of recent U.S. history—
the story of the Cold War—should come tumbling down as well.

We have long been told that the purpose of the U.S. nuclear
force and obscenely large military machine was to "protect" us
from the Soviet Union and its surrogates. Now, with the evil
empire gone, U.S. policymakers have had to search for new enemies to justify maintaining those forces.

We are told Russia remains a threat, though it is not clear what
the threat is or from which segment of that country it might
emerge. China is supposed to worry us as well, though it is not
clear why a nation we court as a major trading partner might want
to wipe us out.

"Rogue states" are also cited as a justification. The most dangerous threat that politicians, military men and weapons-builders
can manage these days is North Korea, which we are told might
have the capacity to build a couple of missiles to deliver conventional weapons. In the words of a *New York Times* reporter, we
face a serious but as yet "unquantifed" threat there.

If the North Koreans can't be sustained as a threat—likely
given that half the population is on the verge of starvation—there
surely will be others targeted. Nicaragua, Panama and Latin
American narcotraffickers, or Iraq, Libya and Islamic terrorists—
all at one time have provided the needed "threat."

In resisting these empty attempts to justify the country's bloated military budgets and nuclear arsenal, however, it is wrong-headed to argue that we no longer need the weapons because the Cold War is over. It is time to face the fact that we never needed them, that the Cold War was constructed by policy-makers not to keep the American public free but to ensure we remained cowed and compliant.

While the Soviets eventually achieved the capacity to destroy us (such is the nature of nuclear weapons), the claim that they were a global military threat to our very existence always had primarily political ends. The Soviet Union was a political threat, which American planners had realized from the 1917 revolution on and had sought to contain at home and abroad. The Soviet regime was authoritarian and brutal, and interventionist in its own sphere. But the main threat was always political—no matter how deformed a version of socialism the Soviets offered, they represented a challenge to the "natural" and "inevitable" domination of business-run societies like the United States, and U.S. business and political leaders were scared.

Though the Cold War was in this sense a myth, it was an amazing propaganda victory that played a very real role in shaping policy. It helped contain what U.S. planners seriously worried about after WWII: the threat of an independent Europe that might remain neutral as the United States tried to squash the Soviet challenge. More than 50 years later, the use of NATO to wage war in the Balkans reminds us of the ongoing success of the project of subordinating Europe to U.S. policy.

At home, the Cold War helped keep the entire nation in fear of the "red menace," making it easier for U.S. officials to repress dissent, maintain a bloated defense budget to increase corporate profits (especially in high-tech industries) through military contracts and pursue a brutal foreign policy that targets virtually all attempts at independent development in the Third World.

The lasting effects of this militarization continue to be felt, at home and abroad. We have spent a total of $5.5 trillion on nuclear weapons, and close to $300 billion a year is drained by the military. About 7,200 nuclear warheads remain deployed, keeping alive the threat of annihilation of the entire planet. Any nation that dares defy U.S. policy risks military or economic assault, or both, in which civilians will be targeted. And all the time it talks about world peace, the United States leads the world in weapons sales.

As we celebrate the exercise of human creativity and freedom that confronted the myths of authoritarian regimes in Eastern Europe and took apart the Berlin Wall a decade ago, we must turn our creativity and freedom toward confronting our myths about the Cold War and taking apart the military machine and the repressive foreign policy that those myths make possible.

That is the task of free citizens in a free society, where no walls can keep us from the truth about ourselves.

Grotesque Comparisons

Although the death toll from economic sanctions in Iraq should engage our consciences, putting that policy on the agenda of not just ordinary Americans but of progressives was a struggle. That's likely the case in part because Saddam Hussein is so easy to demonize, and in part because many people have difficulty understanding that economic sanctions can kill as easily as a military attack.

So, those of us working to get the U.S. government to lift the sanctions tried anything to make clear what the sanctions meant for ordinary people in Iraq. The coincidence that the sanctions were imposed on the same date as the United States dropped the world's first atomic bomb provided an opportunity to take what most people see as a tragedy (even if they continue to defend the dropping of the bomb as necessary to end the war) and use that as an opening to highlight a contemporary tragedy.

In this piece I describe the sanctions as a siege, a term I borrowed from Simon Harak, a Jesuit priest who was one of the leading voices against the sanctions. I highlight this to emphasize, once again, how individual authorship conceals the collective nature of politics. One night in Austin, Harak gave a brilliant talk on the sanctions that was built around the concept of siege. After it was over, I told him I intended to steal his words the next time I spoke or wrote on the subject. He gave his blessing to my rhetorical theft.

As in many of the op/eds in this book, the underlying argument is that U.S. citizens must begin to understand that our government's actions in the international arena cannot be assumed to be just and moral, but must constantly be examined and challenged. That's the task of people of conscience who live in an empire.

Iraq adds its weight to a sad day of remembrance
San Francisco Chronicle, p. 10 (commentary section);
Fort Worth Star-Telegram, August 6, 2000

August 6 marks two anniversaries of death and destruction. One is permanently etched into our collective memory—the flash of light and mushroom cloud over Hiroshima 55 years ago that left as many as 140,000 Japanese dead. To forget the tragedy of the world's first atomic bombing would be a painful moral failure.

The other anniversary concerns death today, death that continues because of an equally painful moral failure. This attack is ongoing, and it has killed far more—at least 1 million innocent people, half of them children under the age of 5, according to UN studies.

For them, death comes not in a flash, but with the slow agony of malnutrition and wasting diseases. The weapon is the ancient tactic of siege, an attack against all living things in a society.

Today marks the 10th anniversary of the attack on Iraq through siege, the imposition of the most comprehensive economic sanctions in modern times. Though administered through the United Nations, the sanctions are the result of U.S. policy and power, of this nation's rejection of the international consensus to lift the siege. The Clinton administration's policy—or what U.S. Rep. David Bonior, D-Mich., has called "infanticide masquerading as policy"—is that sanctions must remain until there is definitive proof that Saddam Hussein's regime is not rebuilding weapons of mass destruction.

Or is the policy that sanctions must remain until Hussein is overthrown? It's hard to tell, because U.S. officials have made both statements, giving Hussein little reason to think he can satisfy the United States.

Whatever the policy, the United States has made it clear that it cares little about the suffering of innocent Iraqis, who live and die with inadequate diets, unclean water that spreads disease and barely functioning medical facilities.

From the point of view of creating and maintaining real peace, U.S. policy is a failure.

Former UN weapons inspector Scott Ritter—hardly an ally of the Iraqis—has called for lifting the sanctions, saying that Iraq is qualitatively disarmed (meaning that the capability to produce or use weapons of mass destruction has been eliminated). But U.S. insistence on quantitative disarmament (accounting for every last weapon or related material) ensures there will be no constructive change.

The sanctions also have done nothing to advance democracy in Iraq. Living on the edge of survival, the Iraqi people have few resources for pressing political change. As Denis Halliday, the former UN humanitarian coordinator in Iraq, notes: "Sanctions will not change governance to democracy. Sanctions encourage isolation, alienation and possibly fanaticism."

But from the point of view of maintaining and extending U.S. power, the policy has worked. What U.S. officials want in Iraq is a government that accepts the iron law of U.S. policy: The resources of the Middle East must remain, as much as possible, under the effective control of the United States. The old colonial model of direct control is gone; now we rely on the cooperation of compliant local governments (authoritarian or democratic; we don't much care) that take their cut and ship most of the remaining profits to the West.

Recalcitrant regimes must be broken so that the flow of oil profits to U.S. and British banks and corporations is not threatened. Iraq, an ally throughout the 1980s until it challenged the U.S. system, is so devastated that it will be decades before it can rebuild.

To oppose the sanctions is not to support the brutal regime of Saddam Hussein, but to reject genocide. That is the term that

Halliday has used, describing the sanctions as an "intentional program to destroy a culture, a people, a country." Rather than stage-manage a genocide, Halliday resigned in protest in 1998. In the past year, his successor, Hans von Sponeck, did the same, as has the director of the World Food Program in Iraq, Jutta Burghardt.

U.S. officials don't feel the same tug of conscience. When interviewed on "60 Minutes" in 1996, Secretary of State Madeline Albright—then U.S. ambassador to the United Nations—was asked if the deaths of a half-million children in Iraq were acceptable. Her answer: "I think this is a very hard choice. But the price—we think the price is worth it."

I do not know by what moral gymnastics Albright reaches such a conclusion.

I do not know how high the death toll in Iraq will climb before U.S. policy changes.

And 55 years from now, I don't know which anniversary of death will weigh most on the consciences of Americans.

Independence Day

This is one of the few pieces included in this book that was commissioned by an editor. Lois Kazakoff, editor of the "Open Forum" pages at the *San Francisco Chronicle*, had run a couple of pieces of mine by the summer of 2000, and we had developed a good email and phone relationship. When she asked about my interest in writing about the Fourth of July, I pitched the piece below to her, and she decided it could fit with her plans for the Sunday opinion section. I was grateful for the opportunity, for it is at a time when most everyone is accepting the conventional wisdom without much thought that we can intervene and suggest a different angle of vision.

I mention this to press the point that radical critics of the news media sometimes go too far in writing off journalists as unthinking minions of the powerful. Journalism is a craft that most journalists take very seriously. No matter how we might critique the craft's professional norms about objectivity and neutrality, we have to realize that the majority of journalists strive to make good on the ideals. They operate in a larger social context that makes it difficult to go too far outside the boundaries of thinkable thought, but there is room in the system for individual journalists to make independent judgments.

I have always found myself eager to get to know the editors I work with, partly because of our shared professional background and partly for purely pragmatic reasons. Not surprisingly, I don't like every editor I encounter. But more often than not I find myself enjoying my work with editors and appreciating the job they do, even when they reject my work.

On Independence Day, hold the self-congratulations
San Francisco Chronicle, July 2, 2000, p. 1 (commentary section);
Houston Chronicle, July 2, 2000, p. 1-C

On bandstands around the country this Fourth of July, politicians will offer heartfelt homilies about "the greatest nation on earth," the United States.

As flags wave in the background, we will tell ourselves a story of the great march of progress the United States has led around the world.

On the day we mark our independence from an old empire, we will talk about the fight for freedom, past and future.

The rhetoric is designed to make Americans feel good about America, but I've always felt uneasy with the Fourth, a holiday allegedly full of a reflective humility yet reflexively self-congratulatory.

This year, the talk of the greatest of nations will ring more hollow to me than ever, because it's become impossible to ignore some painful truths about the United States: The humility is false. The claim of greatness is actually self-deception. The progress has not always been so progressive. The march often has been over the broken bodies of victims whose cries we refuse to hear. And the freedom we claim for ourselves we are too often reluctant to grant to others.

On this Fourth, I will be forced to face a conclusion I have long wanted to avoid: We are the empire, soon to be judged by history the way all empires have been judged, as cruel and self-aggrandizing. If we want to escape that judgment, we as citizens of the empire cannot wait for our leaders or the wealthy to lead us, for theirs is the path to power, not greatness.

This Fourth of July, I believe that citizens of the United States have to commit the ultimate act of patriotism: We must stop being Americans.

By that I don't mean we must give up on the truly noble ideals associated with the United States. Nor do I mean we must turn our backs on the many accomplishments of the people of this country. Nor must we turn our backs on each other. Instead, we must tell the truth about what being an American has come to mean, and we must find a way to rethink and reshape who we are. We are too busy congratulating ourselves; we need to be questioning ourselves.

Such talk may sound strange, especially coming at a time of great triumphalism in the United States. Across the globe our military, political, and economic power is respected or feared, or both. But two questions nag: Would a nation that is truly great want to hoard such power? And how do we use that power? The answers require honest self-reflection about the gap between the values we tell ourselves we hold and the values reflected in our actions, at home and abroad. Such honesty means realizing that unchallenged power and enormous privilege can block us from seeing ourselves and our role in the world clearly.

Some recent vignettes from my life help explain my distress:

• At a political event, I was holding a sign that explained that the economic embargo on Iraq has killed 1 million innocent civilians and asked how many deaths will it take for the United States to abandon our failed policy. A man, an American, walked by, pondered, and said, "I don't know ... how about 2 million?"

• The wealthy American CEO of an Internet company joked at a meeting with employees about his new sport utility vehicle, the biggest on the market. "I bought it,'" he laughed, "because it gets the worst gas mileage."

• A woman from East Timor described to an American audience the beauty of the Timorese countryside but explained that there is no spot left in her country that does not conjure memories of massacres at the hands of the Indonesian invaders. "Do you understand that they have been killing us for more than 20 years with American weapons, with American support?" she asked.

• While walking with a 3-year-old one chilly winter morning, we passed a man sleeping in a doorway. "Why is that man sleeping outside?" the child asked. I had no answer, only another question: Would I have noticed the man if not for the child's question?

Who are we Americans? Who are we to the Iraqi mother who watches her child die in her arms because there is no clean water or adequate food or medicine in her town because of our embargo? Who are we when we slowly choke the planet to death because of self-indulgent consumption that most people around the world find grotesque? Who are we to the survivors in East Timor, rebuilding their lives as they mourn loved ones dead from American weapons, all because we didn't want to disturb profitable business dealings with the conquering Indonesians? Who are we when we step over our brothers and sisters on the street, their pain invisible to us?

What does it mean to be an American in the age of American empire? Can we tell ourselves the truth about that? Is there a mirror that can hold the enormity of that image? And if we do dare to look, where do we go from there?

The politicians and the wealthy are not going to dismantle the empire on their own. It is unlikely they will wake up one morning and suddenly discover a long-misplaced conscience. And if they magically did, the institutions and systems in which they work would not go away. We should expect those with power in the powerful institutions to continue to concentrate even more power in even fewer hands. The rest of us—the vast majority of Americans—face the challenge of forcing change, of making "American" mean something more than callousness, greed, smugness, orgiastic levels of consumption, disregard for the suffering of others and a willingness to kill to protect our privilege and power.

Make no mistake: That is what "American" means to much of the rest of the world. But it need not always mean that. Change is possible. We can start by refusing to repeat the misleading story about our greatness and benevolence. We can stop being loyal citizens of the empire.

The task is not as difficult as it may seem, in part because a portion of the story we tell ourselves is true: We do live in one of the freest societies that has ever existed. We can speak with little fear of retribution. We can organize. We can act.

This Fourth of July, we can challenge the holiday's empty rhetoric. When the politicians talk about being the greatest nation on earth, we can stand up and question the arrogance of such a claim. When they talk about the American commitment to peace, we can ask why the United States leads the world in weapons sales and routinely conducts military operations outside international law. When they talk about the booming economy, we can ask who benefits from the stock market and financial speculation, and who is left behind. Most important, when they tell us that being an American means being loyal to the empire, we can stand up and say, "Enough—I will be an American no longer." Then we can step onto the long road to redefining ourselves.

We have to challenge our own privilege, question our own consumption, ask on whose backs our comfort is built. We have to realize that the things we have won have come with a price, that what we have taken has costs for others, now and for future generations. If we do that with commitment and compassion, it may well turn out we stop worrying about what it means to be an American and start concentrating on what it means to be a human being.

Chapter 8

Getting Personal

It is impossible to write a successful op/ed without being able to make a clear argument backed up with evidence. But sometimes all the evidence and clear reasoning in the world doesn't move editors to run a piece or readers to accept the argument. Telling stories, especially personal stories, can sometimes be effective in a way that straightforward arguments are not.

So, whenever possible I look for anecdotes from my life to make more real the political points I want to advance. Most of the time such stories are difficult to fit in an essay for a public forum, but sometimes a conversation from my life or an observation about my world can crystallize a political point and convey more than traditional arguments.

On the other hand, pieces that lean too heavily on sentiment also can be dangerous. An op/ed that goes too far and gets sappy is unlikely to get published, and if it does run it may well turn off people who sense an attempt to manipulate their emotions. But beyond that, there's a risk that we trivialize core political arguments when we try to play on sentiment. Emotion is, of course, part of politics—I would hope radical politics is always motivated by emotional connections to people and the world. (One is reminded of Che Guevara's memorable comment that "the true revolutionary is guided by great feelings of love.") But it's important that that level of emotion not turn into Hollywood-style sentimentality for the sake of trying to appeal to people.

Simple Truths

I worried a lot about being overly sentimental in this piece that drew on a conversation I had with my son. I wrote it after two years of political organizing on the subject of the brutal U.S.-imposed economic embargo on Iraq, at a time when many of us were terribly frustrated at how little mainstream news coverage there was of the issue. Because there were few changes in the sanctions from day to day, it was difficult to find a news hook for op/eds.

After my son and I had a conversation about the sanctions and he decided to send money to help the people of Iraq, I told the story to several friends, focusing mostly on how we tend to underestimate our children—Luke's level of moral thinking on the issue seemed light years ahead of most adults. As I told the story, I kept thinking, if we all could just think like a 7-year-old. That phrase stuck in my head, and after a few days I realized I had the makings of an op/ed, one that could emphasize how simple moral truths that a kid easily understands make the Iraq issue so clear.

So, I sat down and wrote, trying to draw on the power of my conversation with Luke without turning the piece into a self-indulgent ramble about how great my kid is, or something stupidly sentimental that soft-pedaled the important political points. Readers can evaluate how well I balanced these concerns. But I'm fairly certain that an op/ed that made the same argument without the personal story would not have run in that paper.

After I wrote it, I talked to Luke and asked if he wanted me to try to publish an article in which he was mentioned. I explained what it said, and he told me it was okay with him to put it in the newspaper.

Even a child sees through Iraqi policy
Dallas Morning News, August 27, 1999, p. 29-A

(Note: The headline that the paper used should have read "Iraq policy," meaning the policy of the United States toward Iraq, not the Iraqi's own policy.)

If only all the world had the conscience of a 7-year-old.

For the past two years I have been organizing and speaking out against the war on Iraq that the United States is waging through bombing and economic sanctions. One recent Sunday morning, a colleague and I spoke to a local group and appeared on cable access television about the issue. My 7-year-old son, Luke, sat through both appearances, seemingly more interested in his toys than in three hours of talk about the viciousness of U.S. foreign policy.

But over dinner that night, he started quizzing me about the issue, and it was clear he had been listening.

In the talk, we had explained that nine years of sanctions had crippled the Iraqi economy and were directly responsible for as many as 1 million civilian deaths from malnutrition and disease. On the heels of the devastation of Iraq's health, sanitation and education infrastructure in the 1991 Gulf War, the sanctions were inducing deep poverty and preventing the rebuilding of the country.

Although the U.S. government contends the brutal embargo is in place to force Iraq to comply with weapons inspections, with perhaps the added goal of forcing the Iraqi people to overthrow the Hussein regime, the sanctions' main mission is to send a message to the rest of the world: This is what happens when a country defies the United States—we will destroy you. The U.S. right to dominate the resources of the Middle East, and the rest of the world, cannot be challenged.

In 1996 when interviewed on "60 Minutes," Madeline Albright—then ambassador to the United Nations and now secretary of state—was asked if the deaths of a half-million children in Iraq were an acceptable price to pay for a policy. "I think this is a very hard choice," Albright acknowledged. "But the price—we think the price is worth it."

It is difficult to imagine any policy that is worth the deaths of a half-million children. That those children have died simply to shore up U.S. power is a crime against humanity that is impossible to justify.

If only government officials had the conscience of a 7-year-old.

At dinner, Luke asked questions. He's going to a "normal" public school, where kids are trained to think the U.S. government doesn't kill innocent people. He wants to believe what he is being taught about U.S. benevolence around the world, but he is willing to reject the mythology in light of the facts.

Is the leader of Iraq good? he asked. No, I explained, he is a bad guy who sometimes even hurts his own people, but that doesn't mean the people should suffer even more under sanctions. Why don't the Iraqis get rid of him? he asked. That's complicated,

I said, but right now the people of Iraq spend most of their time trying to stay alive and aren't in a very good position to overthrow a government.

How do sanctions work? Why don't other countries just sell Iraq things that they need? I explained that most of the world would like to see the sanctions lifted, but that the United States has more guns and power than anyone else, and so the United States generally gets what it wants.

Why don't the people in Iraq just come and live here? he asked. When I told him that wasn't possible, he asked if we could send some food and toys to Iraq. I said that the postal service wouldn't let us mail anything of value to Iraq, but that a group in Chicago called Voices in the Wilderness made trips to Iraq and delivered medicine. It would be better to send Voices a donation, I said.

"That's it," Luke said. He ran to get his wallet and emptied out a $10 bill and some coins. "I want to send it all to those people who are helping," he said. I told Luke that he didn't have to donate all his money, that it would be okay to give just some of what he had. But his mind was made up. He gathered together a few small toys to include in the package with the donation, dictated a letter, and drew a picture of himself so that the Voices folks would know who sent it.

I hesitated for a moment: Because Voices in the Wilderness has not sought a license from the U.S. government to take humanitarian supplies to Iraq, the group has been threatened with $163,000 in fines. Technically, Luke could be liable for contributing to that "crime," though I expect the Clinton administration is not so vindictive that they would prosecute elementary-school kids.

Luke's unprompted offer to help was particularly uplifting for me. At protests and talks for the past two years I have been listening to adults who tell me that they don't care about the fate of Iraqis and that they hope that the sanctions squeeze them until Hussein is out, no matter how many innocent people die. Once while at a political event holding up a banner that read, "1 million dead from sanctions—how many will be enough?" a man walked by me, smirked, and said, "I don't know ... how about 2 million?"

If only all Americans had the conscience of a 7-year-old.

———————

Capitalist Values

The IMF/World Bank meeting protests provided the same opening that the WTO protests had for op/eds. It was not only possible to critique those institutions, but to go after the basic rules of the game in capitalism. Much like the piece that targeted the corporate form, this one went after the underlying assumptions about human nature that are inherent in capitalism. The task when doing this in the mainstream is to keep the critique sharp without relying on hackneyed phrases.

In this case, I tried to do that by talking about my own emotional responses to living in a culture that not only accepts the debased notions about human nature in capitalism (that people are motivated primarily by greed and self-interest) but celebrates them. The sadness I discuss in the piece is real, and I feel it every day in different ways. I think acknowledging that early in the piece might have helped keep editors, and readers, engaged.

I suspect that what led to the piece being published was my use of the conversation with the business student that I recount at the end. It was a strangely emotional encounter, especially after being attacked by most of the audience at the forum. I didn't want to make too much of it, but I did want to convey what can happen when one is willing to put oneself out in public. I believe that many of us in the United States carry around a deep sadness about the world we are forced to live in, and I think making visible that sadness and being clear about the sources of it is part of the path to a better future.

In moral accounting, First World's the debtor
Houston Chronicle, April 16, 2000, p. 5-C

As the protests in the streets of Washington, DC, unfold on Sunday at the International Monetary Fund and the World Bank meeting, the focus will be on complex fiscal and monetary policy questions. But the underlying struggle is over more basic questions:

What is an economy for, and what does it mean to be a human being in the modern world?

Is an economy simply a system and set of institutions to maximize production no matter what the cost to people and the planet? Or should the goal of an economy be to create conditions under which free human beings can tap their creative potential and work collectively to fashion a sustainable world?

Is money the only measure of value, or does real wealth come from the living capital of the planet?

Do we judge an economy solely on market values? Or do solidarity, compassion and love have a place—not just in our families and intimate lives, but in public as well, in the way we collectively define ourselves? These issues arose when a political colleague and I recently debated two business school professors on the question of corporate responsibility.

During the discussion, I talked about the sadness that I so often feel living in a society in which such human values are not only marginalized but mocked because they are inconsistent with the demands of the economy. The most vulnerable—the poor, children, the aged, the sick—suffer most from this state of affairs. But we all suffer because the conception of human nature inherent in our economy is so debased.

Make no mistake: The view of human nature that underlies corporate capitalism is inhumane and antihuman. We are told that people will respond only to crass self-interest and greed, and hence our economic institutions are built on that notion. Then, when people often do act on self-interest and greed in a system that rewards such behavior, we are told, "See, look at how greedy people are."

It is our task not to accept such facile logic, to reject former British Prime Minister Margaret Thatcher's famous dictate "There is no alternative." There are, of course, alternatives. There is nothing natural or inevitable about capitalism and its underlying assertions about human nature.

We all have experienced situations in which we put aside crass calculations about self-interest and acted out of a sense of solidarity, an understanding that to be fully human means meaningful connection with others. We also all have been, at some time, selfish and greedy. Both are part of human nature. The question is, do we build institutions that encourage our capacity for kindness or for cruelty?

An economy is the product of human choices. By definition, we can choose differently. For example, we can choose to eliminate IMF and World Bank lending policies that undercut education, health, and social services in the developing world in order to maximize profits in the developed world. We can simply abandon these "structural adjustment" policies, which adjust the lives of ordinary people downward.

We can realize that a minimal sense of justice means the First World must forgive the debt it has imposed on the Third World and begin to talk about a real moral accounting for colonialism through the First World paying reparations.

And, when our collective moral imagination has developed enough, we can begin to design a world in which corporations are not allowed to trample over people in pursuit of profits.

That world may not be as far away as we think. After our business school debate, an MBA student came up to me and thanked us for being willing to speak before a group that was so hostile to our message.

"I don't agree with everything you said, and I am going to go into business," he told me. Then his voice wavered a bit, and he said, "But what you said touched me."

That moment—a connection between two people, standing in a building constructed to teach people to honor greed—touched me as well. It was a reminder of those other values, of the possibility of alternatives. The only question is whether together we have the courage to create them.

———————

Chapter 9

Counteroffensives

One opportunity to inject radical opinions into the mainstream comes when local organizing is covered, or miscovered, by the local paper. Some of these problems can be remedied by a correction written by the newspaper, or a letter to the editor from the activist. But if a paper makes egregious errors in reporting or in editorials, and especially if it makes them consistently over time, activists can sometimes argue that out of fairness we deserve op/ed space to respond.

Of course, the editors make the final determination of when their own mistakes require such an offer of space, and such offers are rare. But activists should push for them when openings occur. And, as is always the case, the failure to get space to respond at one point in time doesn't mean the effort was wasted. Often it is the cumulative pressure that brings the desired results somewhere down the road.

Speaking of Henry Kissinger

That situation happened in Austin after a controversy about the cancellation of a speech by Henry Kissinger because of protests being planned. From the beginning, the paper's coverage in the news section accepted the university administration's line that a bunch of dangerous radicals on campus might have created a threat to public safety by protesting Kissinger's talk. Such coverage that parrots official sources is hardly surprising; even when reporters talked to those of us who were organizing the protest and heard our side, the stories still generally accepted the officials' framework.

However, when the local paper wrote an editorial that repeated the same unfounded claims, included a couple of fact errors, and condemned me by name, it was clear we had a good case for demanding space. So, I got on the phone to the editor of the editorial pages and asked for a correction of the fact errors and space to respond. He hesitated a bit but didn't argue; I think his own instincts to be fair kicked in, and he agreed.

"How much space do we get?" I asked. He called up the editorial on his computer and ran a word count.

"How does 577 words sound?" he said. I laughed and said it sounded just fine. So, I sat down with Rahul Mahajan, one of the leaders of the student group that planned the protest, and we began writing. When I did the final edit, the piece was 585 words. Just for fun, I found eight words to cut.

After the piece ran in the Austin paper, I sent it to other papers in the state, which often pick up on UT stories, and the Houston paper also ran it. That's a reminder of what I tell my students is one of the basic rules of freelancing: Sell everything you write, and sell it as often as possible.

The real threat to free speech at UT
Austin American-Statesman, February 4, 2000, p. A-15;
Houston Chronicle, February 9, 2000, p. 31-A

by Rahul Mahajan and Robert Jensen

In truly Orwellian fashion, University of Texas officials and a recent *American-Statesman* editorial have tried to paint UT student activists' attempts to promote spirited political debate as an attack on free speech.

When the director of the LBJ Library announced that he had advised Henry Kissinger to cancel his planned Feb. 1 lecture, we were accused by UT's chancellor and president of "threatening to endanger public safety" through the use of "immoral" tactics. These charges are, quite frankly, silly, as the failure of these officials to give evidence of the threat or even specify the nature of the danger reveals. Not surprisingly, our invitation to the officials for a public debate about the issues has been rejected.

We have helped organize dozens of political protests and forums in Austin in the past two years, none of which have been violent; this one would have been no different. We did not plan to suppress anyone's speech. Instead, we wanted to engage in free speech by distributing literature that highlighted Kissinger's crimes and by talking to people at the event.

More important, we wanted Kissinger to speak, and in fact speak more than he usually does in response to tough questions about his role in the subversion of democracy and violations of international law around the world. We wanted to ask him what he said to Gen. Suharto in a meeting two days before the Indonesian dictator used U.S.-supplied weapons to begin the genocide in East Timor in 1975. Why did he work so hard to undermine the democratically elected government of Chile in the 1970s? How does he feel knowing that hundreds of thousands of Cambodians died in the "secret" war he planned there in 1969?

We planned to do what citizens in a democracy have a right, and a moral obligation, to do—hold someone who made policy accountable for his decisions. Free speech does not mean a free ride for policymakers who support dictators, genocide and illegal wars.

Charges that we restricted Kissinger's speech are ludicrous. It was LBJ Library officials who cut off his opportunity to speak using manufactured fears of threats to public safety. Furthermore, Kissinger is not lacking in opportunities to speak, especially through the mass media.

Political dissidents do not get the ongoing opportunities to be heard at great length that Kissinger enjoys. That is why we use face-to-face discussion, civil disobedience and protest, strategies that have won many of the civil rights we now take for granted. Such protests are much admired by people in power—in theory, and as long as they are comfortably in the past. But if we use peaceful protest effectively in the present, it is likely that police violence will be unleashed, as it was against nonviolent protesters in Seattle.

We take seriously the role of a university, not simply to tolerate political discourse but to promote it actively. For democracy to be meaningful, political discourse must be critical of powerful people and institutions. The late Supreme Court Justice William Brennan said it best in a landmark free-speech case: Such debate must be "uninhibited, robust, and wide-open" and "may well include vehement, caustic, and sometimes unpleasantly sharp attacks on government and public officials."

The UT administration has shown that it is ready to fabricate charges in order to demonize dissent, a dangerous sign. The *American-Statesman*'s editorial uncritically passed along these distortions. The chilling effect of such developments is the real threat to free speech.

———————————

Chapter 10

Personal Connections and Dumb Luck

This story is a reminder to the world that writing has power, and that every one of us has within us the power to write and to touch other people. It's also a story about how luck and connections don't hurt.

The story starts a few years ago, when I was sitting at a college cafeteria table with Laird Anderson, a professor from my master's program in journalism and public affairs at American University, trading gossip and speculating about fates and futures. I had just received tenure in my university teaching job, which meant I had a level of job security and freedom rare in the contemporary workplace.

I told Laird that I was going to move out of scholarly writing for specialized audiences and try to get back to more journalistic writing, especially for mainstream papers. Though Laird's politics are very different from mine, he endorsed the idea and encouraged me to contact another former student who had completed the same program a few years after me. Mike Adams was editor of the Sunday "Perspective" section of the *Baltimore Sun*, Laird said, and he often used freelance writers.

When I got home, I gave Mike a call and told him about my conversation with Laird. He asked me what kinds of pieces I had in mind, and I told him about some of my interests. "Do you have anything in the works at the moment?" he asked.

I did. Sitting in my computer for the past year had been an essay about race, racism, and white privilege that I had written in reaction to a nasty political battle over affirmative action at the University of Texas. Would he like to take a look at it? Sure, he said. No guarantees, but he would read it.

That simple exchange set in motion a series of events that has led to that essay being published and widely circulated, more writing, appearances on television and radio talk shows, and speaking engagements all over the country. The piece ran in the *Baltimore Sun* and then in other papers around the country that took it off the *L.A. Times/Washington Post* wire. From there, it was downloaded off newspaper Web sites and databases, and circulated via email and Internet discussion lists.

That first 1,600-word essay struck a chord in people in a way I could never have predicted, and in some sense still don't quite understand. In three years, I have received about 1,000 letters and emails in response to the original piece, the follow-up essay that ran a year later, and other writings on the subject. It seems strange that a piece that had the simple thesis that white people living in a white-supremacist society have certain privileges by virtue of their skin color (hardly a revolutionary concept) could spark such a response. I have re-read the pieces countless times, and I still don't find them particularly compelling myself. I do not think they are the best writing I have ever done. I continue to ask myself, why the intensity of interest in them?

The answer is probably that in a world in which there is so much coded, defensive, scared, self-serving, and dishonest writing by white people about race, a simple attempt to think about the problem of racism in public was refreshing to people. Instead of pointing fingers at others, I tried to talk honestly about personal accountability in a system that is so obviously unjust. I didn't pretend racism was a problem located "out there" but instead wrote about how it lives in me and in my world. I offered no grand theory to account for it and didn't pretend to have easy answers.

In this story, there are important lessons for anyone who wants to write.

First, I was not, and am not, an expert on race. My own scholarly work has touched on race, but I am by no means a scholar of race. In the pieces, I made no claim to expertise or special status from which to speak. I wrote as a person and a citizen who was struggling, and continues to struggle, with difficult questions about race and racism, in society and in myself. Experts sometimes have important contributions to make to such public debates. Citizens always have such contributions.

Second, I didn't fall prey to thinking that whatever I might say had already been said better by someone else. Certainly there is no shortage of writing about race out there, much of it more thoughtful and insightful than my pieces. Peggy McIntosh's piece on "White Privilege and Male Privilege," which covers much the same ground, has been widely anthologized and read. But one can never tell what effect any single piece of writing might have on people. It's not just the content, but the tone and timing of an article that can determine its fate in the mind of a reader.

Finally, while it would be wonderful if we lived in a world in which merit alone determined who was successful, the fact is that personal connections to editors can be important. If I had submitted that essay to the *Sun* editor without benefit of our college connection, he still might have run it. Or, in the crush of an editor's busy work week, he might never have gotten a chance to read it with care. Writers are never really sure how whether manuscripts that are submitted cold actually get read.

So, don't be shy about following any and all leads that could connect you with an editor. So long as the work is good, the chances that your writing will be published go up dramatically when the editor who reads it knows your name. Don't be afraid to explore such connections, but keep interaction at an appropriately professional level.

To follow up on the essay, I asked the editor whether he would be interested in a piece on a specific criminal case in Austin that I had wanted to write about for some time. This would be not simply an opinion piece but would include reporting on the case. I designed the article on Lacresha Murray to raise questions about the fairness of her trials and spark attention outside of Austin. It also was a case that illustrated how race and class bias exist in the system, even when there is no overt discrimination. After that, I wrote another piece at Mike's suggestion (on gun control, which is not included in this book) before returning to the subject of white privilege in a follow-up article based on the mail I had received about the piece.

Mike hasn't taken every piece I have written (a third piece on race and another on U.S. policy toward Iraq were rejected), but that's to be expected. A few months after those rejections, I came back to him with a different piece on U.S. policy in Iraq, which was a better fit for his section and that he did publish. Although there is a personal connection, I approach Mike as a professional who will expect certain things from me, as he would any writer. The result has been productive for me. Even when he rejects a piece, Mike gives me candid assessments that help me improve my work.

White privilege shapes the U.S.
Baltimore Sun, July 19, 1998, p. C-1

Here's what white privilege sounds like:

I am sitting in my University of Texas office, talking to a very bright and very conservative white student about affirmative action in college admissions, which he opposes and I support.

The student says he wants a level playing field with no un-earned advantages for anyone. I ask him whether he thinks that in the United States being white has advantages. Have either of us, I ask, ever benefited from being white in a world run mostly by white people? Yes, he concedes, there is something real and tangi-ble we could call white privilege.

So, if we live in a world of white privilege—unearned white privilege—how does that affect your notion of a level playing field? I ask.

He paused for a moment and said, "That really doesn't matter."

That statement, I suggested to him, reveals the ultimate white privilege: the privilege to acknowledge you have unearned privi-lege but ignore what it means.

That exchange led me to rethink the way I talk about race and racism with students. It drove home to me the importance of confronting the dirty secret that we white people carry around with us everyday: In a world of white privilege, some of what we have is unearned. I think much of both the fear and anger that comes up around discussions of affirmative action has its roots in that secret. So these days, my goal is to talk openly and honestly about white supremacy and white privilege.

White privilege, like any social phenomenon, is complex. In a white supremacist culture, all white people have privilege, whether or not they are overtly racist themselves. There are gen-eral patterns, but such privilege plays out differently depending on context and other aspects of one's identity (in my case, being male gives me other kinds of privilege). Rather than try to tell others how white privilege has played out in their lives, I talk about how it has affected me.

I am as white as white gets in this country. I am of northern European heritage and I was raised in North Dakota, one of the whitest states in the country. I grew up in a virtually all-white world surrounded by racism, both personal and institutional. Because I didn't live near a reservation, I didn't even have exposure to the state's only numerically significant nonwhite population, American Indians.

I have struggled to resist that racist training and the ongoing racism of my culture. I like to think I have changed, even though I routinely trip over the lingering effects of that internalized racism and the institutional racism around me. But no matter how much I "fix" myself, one thing never changes—I walk through the world with white privilege.

What does that mean? Perhaps most importantly, when I seek admission to a university, apply for a job, or hunt for an apartment, I don't look threatening. Almost all of the people evaluating me for those things look like me—they are white. They see in me a reflection of themselves, and in a racist world that is an advantage. I smile. I am white. I am one of them. I am not dangerous. Even when I voice critical opinions, I am cut some slack. After all, I'm white.

My flaws also are more easily forgiven because I am white. Some complain that affirmative action has meant the university is saddled with mediocre minority professors. I have no doubt there are minority faculty who are mediocre, though I don't know very many. As Henry Louis Gates Jr. once pointed out, if affirmative action policies were in place for the next hundred years, it's possible that at the end of that time the university could have as many mediocre minority professors as it has mediocre white professors. That isn't meant as an insult to anyone, but is a simple observation that white privilege has meant that scores of second-rate white professors have slid through the system because their flaws were overlooked out of solidarity based on race, as well as on gender, class and ideology.

Some people resist the assertions that the United States is still a bitterly racist society and that the racism has real effects on real people. But white folks have long cut other white folks a break. I know, because I am one of them.

I am not a genius—as I like to say, I'm not the sharpest knife in the drawer. I have been teaching full-time for six years, and I've published a reasonable amount of scholarship. Some of it is the unexceptional stuff one churns out to get tenure, and some of it, I would argue, actually is worth reading. I work hard, and I like to think that I'm a fairly decent teacher. Every once in awhile, I leave my office at the end of the day feeling like I really accomplished something. When I cash my paycheck, I don't feel guilty.

But, all that said, I know I did not get where I am by merit alone. I benefited from, among other things, white privilege. That doesn't mean that I don't deserve my job, or that if I weren't white I would never have gotten the job. It means simply that all through my life, I have soaked up benefits for being white. I grew up in fertile farm country taken by force from nonwhite indigenous people. I was educated in a well-funded, virtually all-white public school system in which I learned that white people like me made this country great. There I also was taught a variety of skills, including how to take standardized tests written by and for white people.

All my life I have been hired for jobs by white people. I was accepted for graduate school by white people. And I was hired for a teaching position at the predominantly white University of Texas, which had a white president, in a college headed by a white dean, and in a department with a white chairman that at the time had one nonwhite tenured professor.

There certainly is individual variation in experience. Some white people have had it easier than me, probably because they came from wealthy families that gave them even more privilege. Some white people have had it tougher than me because they came from poorer families. White women face discrimination I will never know. But, in the end, white people all have drawn on white privilege somewhere in their lives.

Like anyone, I have overcome certain hardships in my life. I have worked hard to get where I am, and I work hard to stay there. But to feel good about myself and my work, I do not have to believe that "merit," as defined by white people in a white country, alone got me here. I can acknowledge that in addition to all that hard work, I got a significant boost from white privilege, which continues to protect me every day of my life from certain hardships.

At one time in my life, I would not have been able to say that, because I needed to believe that my success in life was due solely to my individual talent and effort. I saw myself as the heroic American, the rugged individualist. I was so deeply seduced by the culture's mythology that I couldn't see the fear that was binding me to those myths. Like all white Americans, I was living with the fear that maybe I didn't really deserve my success, that maybe luck and privilege had more to do with it than brains and hard work. I was afraid I wasn't heroic or rugged, that I wasn't special.

I let go of some of that fear when I realized that, indeed, I wasn't special, but that I was still me. What I do well, I still can take pride in, even when I know that the rules under which I work in are stacked in my benefit. I believe that until we let go of the fiction that people have complete control over their fate—that we can will ourselves to be anything we choose—then we will live with that fear. Yes, we should all dream big and pursue our dreams and not let anyone or anything stop us. But we all are the product both of what we will ourselves to be and what the society in which we live lets us be.

White privilege is not something I get to decide whether or not I want to keep. Every time I walk into a store at the same time as a black man and the security guard follows him and leaves me alone to shop, I am benefiting from white privilege. There is not space here to list all the ways in which white privilege plays out in our daily lives, but it is clear that I will carry this privilege with me until the day white supremacy is erased from this society.

Frankly, I don't think I will live to see that day; I am realistic about the scope of the task. However, I continue to have hope, to believe in the creative power of human beings to engage the world honestly and act morally. A first step for white people, I think, is to not be afraid to admit that we have benefited from white privilege. It doesn't mean we are frauds who have no claim to our success. It means we face a choice about what we do with our success.

Robert Jensen

More thoughts on why system of white privilege is wrong
Baltimore Sun, July 4, 1999, p. C-1

(Note: Editors at the *Sun* made several changes to the first paragraphs of this essay, and it ran in the *Sun* with those changes. The version below is my original; I like it better.)

By writing about the politics of white privilege—and listening to the folks who responded to that writing—I have had to face one more way that privilege runs deep in my life, and it makes me uncomfortable.

The discomfort tells me I might be on the right track.

Last year I published an article about white privilege in the *Baltimore Sun* that then went out over a wire service to other newspapers. Electronic copies proliferated and were picked up on Internet discussion lists, and the article took on a life of its own.

As a result, every week over the past year I have received at least a dozen letters from people who want to talk about race. I learned not only more about my own privilege, but more about why many white folks can't come to terms with the truism I offered in that article: White people, whether overtly racist or not, benefit from living in a world mostly run by white people that has been built on the land and the backs of nonwhite people.

The reactions varied from racist rantings, to deeply felt expressions of pain and anger, to declarations of solidarity. But probably the most important response I got was from nonwhite folks, predominantly African-Americans, who said something like this: "Of course there is white privilege. I've been pointing it out to my white friends and coworkers for years. Isn't it funny that almost no one listens to me, but everyone takes notice when a white guy says it."

Those comments forced me again to ponder the privilege I live with. Who really does know more about white privilege, me or the people on the other side of that privilege? Me, or a black inner-city teenager who is automatically labeled a gang member and feared by many white folks? Me, or an American Indian on the streets of a U.S. city who is invisible to many white folks? Whose voices should we be paying attention to?

My voice gets heard in large part because I am a white man with a Ph.D. who holds a professional job with status. In most settings, I speak with the assumption that people not only will listen, but will take me seriously. I speak with the assumption that my motives will not be challenged; I can rely on the perception of me as a neutral authority, someone whose observations can be trusted.

Every time I open my mouth, I draw on, and in some ways reinforce, my privilege, which is in large part tied to race.

Right now, I want to use that privilege to acknowledge the many nonwhite people who took the time to tell me about the enduring realities of racism in the United States. And, I want to talk to the white people who I think misread my essay and misunderstand what's at stake.

The responses of my white critics broke down into a few basic categories, around the following claims:

1. White privilege doesn't exist because affirmative action has made being white a disadvantage. The simple response: Extremely limited attempts to combat racism, such as affirmative action, do virtually nothing to erase the white privilege built over 500 years that pervades our society. As a friend of mine says, the only real disadvantage to being white is that it so often prevents people from understanding racial issues.

2. White privilege exists, but it can't be changed because it is natural for any group to favor its own, and besides, the worst manifestations of racism are over. Response: This approach makes human choices appear outside of human control, which is a dodge to avoid moral and political responsibility for the injustice we continue to live with.

3. White privilege exists, and that's generally been a good thing because white Europeans have civilized the world. Along the way some bad things may have happened, and we should take care to be nice to nonwhites to make up for that. Response: These folks often argued the curiously contradictory position that (1) nonwhites and their cultures are not inferior, but (2) white/European culture is superior. As for the civilizing effect of Europe, we might consider five centuries of inhuman, brutal

colonialism and World Wars I and II, and then ask what "civilized" means.

4. White privilege exists because whites are inherently superior, and I am a weakling and a traitor for suggesting otherwise. Response: The Klan isn't dead.

There is much to say beyond those short responses, but for now I am more interested in one common assumption that all these correspondents made, that my comments on race and affirmative action were motivated by "white liberal guilt." The problem is, they got two out of the three terms wrong. I am white, but I'm not a liberal. In political terms, I'm a radical; I don't think liberalism offers real solutions because it doesn't attack the systems of power and structures of illegitimate authority that are the root cause of oppression, be it based on race, gender, sexuality, or class. These systems of oppression, which are enmeshed and interlocking, require radical solutions.

And I don't feel guilty. Guilt is appropriate when one has wronged another, when one has something to feel guilty about. In my life I have felt guilty for racist or sexist things I have said or done, even when they were done unconsciously. But that is guilt I felt because of specific acts, not for the color of my skin. Also, focusing on individual guilt feelings is counterproductive when it leads us to ponder the issue from a psychological point of view instead of a moral and political one.

So, I cannot, and indeed should not, feel either guilty or proud about being white, because it is a state of being I have no control over. However, as a member of a society—and especially as a privileged member of society—I have an obligation not simply to enjoy that privilege that comes with being white but to study and understand it, and work toward a more just world in which such unearned privilege is eliminated.

Some of my critics said that such a goal is ridiculous; after all, people have unearned privileges of all kinds. Several people pointed out that tall people, for example, have unearned privilege in basketball, and we don't ask tall people to stop playing basketball nor do we eliminate their advantage.

The obvious difference is that racial categories are invented; they carry privilege or disadvantage only because people with power create and maintain the privilege for themselves at the expense of others. The privilege is rooted in violence and is maintained through that violence as well as through more subtle means.

I can't change the world so that everyone is the same height, so that everyone has the same shot at being a pro basketball player. In fact, I wouldn't want to; it would be a drab and boring world if we could erase individual differences like that. But I can work with others to change the world to erase the effects of differences that have been created by one group to keep others down.

Not everyone who wrote to me understood this. In fact, the most creative piece of mail I received in response to the essay also was the most confused. In a padded envelope from Clement, Minn., came a brand-new can of Kiwi Shoe Polish, black. Because there was no note or letter, I have to guess at my correspondent's message, but I assume the person was suggesting that if I felt so bad about being white, I might want to make myself black.

But, of course, I don't feel bad about being white. The only motivation I might have to want to be black—to be something I am not—would be pathological guilt over my privilege. In these matters, guilt is a coward's way out, an attempt to avoid the moral and political questions. As I made clear in the original essay, there is no way to give up the privilege; the society we live in confers it upon us, no matter what we want.

So, I don't feel guilty about being white in a white-supremacist society, but I feel an especially strong moral obligation to engage in collective political activity to try to change the society because I benefit from the injustice. I try to be reflective and accountable, though I am human and I make mistakes. I think a lot about how I may be expressing racism unconsciously, but I don't lay awake at night feeling guilty. Guilt is not a particularly productive emotion, and I don't wallow in it.

What matters is what we decide to do with the privilege. For me, that means speaking, knowing that I speak with a certain unearned privilege that gives me advantages I cannot justify. It also means learning to listen before I speak, and realizing that I am probably not as smart as I sometimes like to think I am.

It means listening when an elderly black man who sees the original article tacked up on the bulletin board outside my office while on a campus tour stops to chat. This man, who has lived with more kinds of racism than I can imagine through more decades than I have been alive, says to me: "White privilege, yes, good to keep an eye on that, son. Keep yourself honest. But don't forget to pay attention to the folks who live without the privilege."

It doesn't take black shoe polish to pay attention. It takes only a bit of empathy to listen, and a bit of courage to act.

Justice goes unserved for a Texas girl; Class, race emerge in child's conviction for a toddler's death
Baltimore Sun, September 13, 1998, p. 1N

How deeply do the politics of race and class continue to haunt the U.S. criminal justice system? A Texas murder case gives us hints:

Lacresha Murray reads over the statement that two Austin, Texas, police detectives want her to sign concerning the death of 2-year-old Jayla Belton.

Lacresha hasn't seen her family in four days. She is alone, with no attorney, parent or guardian.

She is black. She is from a working-class neighborhood. She is 11 years old.

After consistently saying that she didn't hurt Jayla, Lacresha agrees with the detectives that she might have accidentally dropped and kicked the baby while taking her to get help. Then Lacresha struggles to read the statement they want her to sign. She stops at a word she doesn't understand.

"What's that word? Home-a-seed?" she asks.

The detective corrects her pronunciation: "Homicide."

"What's that?" Lacresha asks. The question goes unanswered. She continues to read. The detectives had told her that they were just trying to help her and her family, that she could go home once things were straightened out.

Lacresha signs the statement, but she doesn't go home.

Two years later, after a conviction based almost entirely on that statement—what one of Lacresha's attorneys has called an "extracted 'confession'"—Lacresha Murray has yet to go home. She is serving a 25-year sentence.

Police and prosecutors say they did their jobs in a tough case. Critics say Lacresha is a prisoner of the politics of race and class. But no matter what one thinks about Lacresha's guilt or innocence, serious questions about the fairness of her trials remain unanswered.

An appeals court might resolve some of the legal questions in the coming months. But whatever the outcome, one simple question hangs in the air:

Would the police have dared treat a middle- or upper-class white kid the way they treated Lacresha?

That question illustrates the complexity of the intersection of race and class, not only in the criminal justice system but in society more generally. No one suggests that ugly, KKK-style racism was at work. One of the detectives who interrogated Lacresha is Hispanic. The lead prosecutor is black. The district attorney is a Texas liberal who has a history of emphasizing social, not just punitive, solutions to crime.

The district attorney says the case would not have been handled differently in any other part of town. But the organizer of a Lacresha support network argues that "if she had been blond, blue-eyed, in a pinafore, from west Austin [a white, affluent part of town], the police would have never targeted her as a suspect."

In some respects, this case resembles the recent Chicago investigation in which 7- and 8-year-old boys from a predominantly black, low-income community became the youngest children ever charged with murder. The charges were dropped weeks later when police discovered semen on the underwear of the 11-year-old victim and concluded that an adult had to have been involved.

Like the rush to judgment in Chicago, Lacresha's story tells us much about how privilege, or the lack of it, can affect justice, or the lack of it, in the United States.

Lacresha's story began on May 24, 1996, when Jayla Belton was left at the home of Lacresha's grandparents, who are also her adoptive parents and who often would baby-sit Jayla. The 2-year-old had been sick all day, throwing up several times and sleeping most of the day. Later in the afternoon, Lacresha brought Jayla to her grandfather, who realized the seriousness of the child's condition and took her to the hospital. Shortly after their arrival, Jayla was dead.

After an autopsy the next day, the medical examiner ruled the cause of death to be a blow to the liver. Because of the medical examiner's guess about the time of the beating, police focused on the Murray home and Lacresha.

Officials have claimed that the legal requirement that a magistrate grant permission for the questioning of a child didn't apply because Lacresha was not technically in custody at the time detectives interviewed her. Yet Lacresha was read her rights (though it is not clear how much she understood), and the interview tape suggests police were trying to squeeze out a confession.

A week after Jayla's death, Travis County District Attorney Ronnie Earle charged Lacresha with capital murder, telling a news conference that the case showed "that Austin is not immune from the hideous malady sweeping the country of children killing other children."

Lacresha was too young to be charged as an adult; the minimum age for such a charge in Texas is 14. But Earle invoked a sentencing law that can result in a juvenile's being sent to adult prison at age 18 to serve the rest of a fixed sentence.

In August 1996, a jury returned a guilty verdict on charges of intentional injury to a child and criminally negligent homicide, and Lacresha was sentenced to 20 years. Prosecutors acknowledged there was no physical evidence or eyewitness testimony to implicate Lacresha. The state's case rested almost entirely on the statement and shaky circumstantial evidence. Her court-appointed attorney presented no evidence at the trial, believing that the state's case was so weak that the jury would have to acquit.

In October 1996, state District Judge John Dietz threw out the results of the trial over which he had presided, saying he did not think justice had been done.

A second trial in February 1997 resulted in a conviction on the charge of injury to a child. Lacresha was given a 25-year sentence. Her conviction is on appeal to the state's 3rd Court of Appeals. *(Note: In 1999 the appeals court overturned the conviction of Lacresha and she was released from custody.)*

Earle said the investigation of the case was more than adequate and the prosecution was fair. But several holes and contradictions remain in the case. Independent medical examiners and a psychologist have offered compelling rebuttals to prosecution claims in the case. The dropping-and-kicking scenario doesn't fit the severity of the injuries, and despite their efforts in the interrogation, the detectives never got Lacresha to "confess" to more than that.

Also, there was no physical evidence at the Murray home, though the kind of beating Jayla endured likely would have left traces, such as blood. Indications that Jayla might have been beaten elsewhere, before being brought to the Murray home, were not aggressively investigated. Finally, the prosecution never established that Lacresha could have inflicted such a savage beating or had any reason to want to kill the child.

At the time of Jayla's death, several high-profile murder cases with child defendants had captured the nation's attention. And for several years, the news had been full of stories about the alleged increase in violence by children, with some kids labeled "super predators." In such an atmosphere, selling the public on the idea that an 11-year-old girl—especially from a poor side of town occupied largely by minorities—could commit such a brutal crime, even without evidence, proved amazingly easy.

Also at that time, Earle, the long-time Democratic district attorney, was facing an unusually tough election challenge by a Republican. Critics say Earle, who went on to win the race, cynically exploited the Murray case to paint himself as a candidate who was tough on crime. Earle denied that politics played any role and called the public concern about the case "absolutely rabid, runaway goofy" based on a "huge amount of misinformation."

One of those critics, Barbara Taft, started a Lacresha support group, People of the Heart, that has made international connections through its Web site (www.peopleoftheheart.org). Taft, who has worked most of her life as a legal secretary, believes that it will take public pressure to get the legal system to do the right thing.

Even people who say they are unsure of Lacresha's guilt or innocence are disturbed by the way the case was handled by police and prosecutors.

So the question remains: Were Lacresha's race and class a factor in how police perceived the case and how prosecutors shaped the case for the jury? My conclusion is, without question, yes.

Until a friend invited me to attend an informational meeting on the case this spring, I knew nothing more about Lacresha Murray than what I remembered from the local newspaper's coverage. But as I read more and more about the case, my doubts about the conviction deepened.

When I listened to the tape of the police interrogation of Lacresha, I was appalled at how she was bullied and manipulated. Taft describes the interrogation as "immoral, illegal and inadmissible." After reviewing the case, one of Murray's lawyers said the police used "the very best Gestapo tactics" to extract a confession. My conclusion is that a case based on that statement is no case at all.

Like an increasing number of people in Austin, I could no longer believe that Lacresha was responsible for Jayla's death nor defend the behavior of police and prosecutors. As a parent, I know that my child would never have to endure that kind of treatment because he would be protected by his being white and a member of a middle-class, professional family. It is difficult to review the facts of the case and not be sad, angry or both.

The sadness and anger are not only over Lacresha's fate. As Taft reminds people, Jayla's death should also weigh on our consciences. Both girls, she said, were victims of child abuse—Jayla at the hands of an abuser who has gone unpunished, and Lacresha at the hands of the criminal justice system.

"This is not just about racism and classism. We're a society in total denial about the extent of child abuse, and it's the silence of the community that allows that," said Taft, who was physically abused as a child.

"No one spoke for me when I was a child. No one spoke for Jayla when she was alive," Taft said. "That's why we have to speak for Lacresha, because it's silence that kills."

Chapter 11

The Alternative Press

As I suggested in the introduction, the use and support of the alternative press has to be part of any long-term media strategy for left/progressive/radical activists. While we should always look for ways to use the openings in the mainstream media to put forward facts and analysis that can reach a wider public, we shouldn't ignore the small but crucial independent press. For me, that means subscribing to a wide variety of publications and sometimes giving donations beyond the subscription price to help support operations that invariably operate on a shoestring budget. It also means contributing articles on a regular basis.

One common concern about alternative media is that it amounts to little more than "preaching to the choir." This is wrongheaded on two counts. First, the stories in the alternative press do more than just preach. At its best, the alternative press provides information and analysis that are difficult to find anywhere else and are vital to activists. Most folks don't have the time or resources to do in-depth research, and many of us rely on the alternative press (and, increasingly, alternative sources on the Internet) to keep abreast of the variety of issues of concern. That information may not reach millions of people, but it is extremely valuable to the thousands that it does reach.

But beyond that, preaching to the choir isn't always bad. One of the difficult things about holding radical political views is that one rarely sees these viewpoints validated in the mainstream culture. One of the costs of political dissidence is isolation from the people and wider culture around you. That may sound whiny and self-indulgent, given that dissidents at other times and in other parts of the world have routinely faced torture and death, but it is true that it is hard for many people to persevere in the face of that kind of social isolation.

So, having a place where one feels like part of a choir, even if it is a small choir, is important. Political movements have to offer not only a compelling analysis and policy proposals, but also a sense of identity and connection. Reading an article in the alternative press that validates one's position is important, and that function of independent media should not be denigrated.

Included here are pieces from local, regional, and national publications that reflect my own desire to stay involved with political and media work at all those levels. A couple of the articles include direct criticism of the mainstream media, another important role of the alternative press—to provide a space for the criticism of themselves that corporate media are reluctant to run.

Local Options

Several years ago I got a call from a local labor activist about a group that was meeting to start a local labor paper in town. Such papers, once common in the United States, are a rarity now, and I signed up immediately. The eclectic group of left-wing labor folks had no money, of course, but that didn't stop us from producing a paper—*The Working Stiff Journal*—for three years. An ongoing lack of money and a failure to attract enough new people to the project eventually killed the paper, but we successfully produced and distributed a viable paper for those years. My own participation was somewhat peripheral, but it was an invigorating experience in which I learned a lot and became close to some great people, always one of the benefits of political work.

Most of what I wrote for *The Working Stiff Journal* was produced specifically for that paper. But in the case below, the editorial collective allowed me to publish a piece that I originally had written for the local daily paper but had been rejected. After adding some introductory material to explain the situation, I reproduced exactly what the daily's editor had not found fit to publish.

Austin American-Statesman **editor denies
importance of participatory democracy**
The Working Stiff Journal, April 1999, p. 5

In a column in the March 7 issue of the *Austin American-Statesman*, editor Rich Oppel supported a proposed lease of city-owned land downtown to CSC Financial Services Group, taking some shots along the way at what he called the "antibusiness lobby" in Austin.

Apart from the merits of that particular project, Oppel made some curious claims about the nature of democracy that I thought screamed out for a response. So, I wrote the following opinion piece and submitted it to Oppel. He said thanks but no thanks, citing a column run that week in the *Statesman* by local environmental activist Paul Robbins. In his column, Robbins had mentioned that one problem with the CSC deal was that public input had not been solicited, but the piece concentrated mainly on the land deal itself.

I thought a more complete defense of public participation in government was necessary. Oppel didn't agree, suggesting that Robbins's column had adequately represented what Oppel described to me as "that classically Austin way of looking at things."

Funny, but I thought active public participation in civic affairs was supposed to be a classically American way of looking at things. Whatever the origins of the notion that the public has a right to participate in public decision-making, *The Working Stiff Journal* agreed to provide the space for a fuller exploration of the issue than the *Statesman* thought necessary.

Should citizens stay silent on the sidelines while politicians and business people cut deals about how public property is used and who pays the bills? Below is my answer to that question.

Democracy happens outside the voting booth

One of the most important issues to debate in a democracy is the question, "What constitutes democracy?" The discussion is not a self-indulgent waste of time but is in fact crucial to the ongoing struggle to realize the possibility of self-government. Editor Rich Oppel's March 7 column provides an interesting launching pad for the discussion.

In the column about a business relocating to downtown Austin, Oppel presented one view of what democracy is. Deriding those who ask for public hearings on such public matters, Oppel argued that hearings "are influenced by people with no jobs and strong bladders" who can sit in meeting rooms well into the night. Suggesting that hearings are not the "grand democratic process" that some think, Oppel explained that "the core of democracy in representative government occurs in the election booth."

In this analysis, Oppel follows a long line of U.S. political theory that extols the inherent virtue of managers and experts. Unfortunately, in the name of promoting democracy, the theory is the death of democracy.

The argument usually goes something like this: Modern industrial societies are too complex for the average person to understand. Hence, policy decisions must be left in the hands of an elite class of experts—politicians, social scientists, policy wonks, and so on. These people, the responsible folks, should be given the task of working out the best solutions for us all.

From this view, the public has a role, which Oppel describes correctly. Every few years, our duty is to trudge off to the polls and select which gang of experts we want to make the real decisions. Once we've pulled the levers for our candidates, our job is done, and we can all trudge home, flip on the tube, and enjoy ourselves, safe in the knowledge that our trusted public servants are doing their best.

On occasion those trusted servants may make mistakes, which is where Oppel's enterprise comes in: Another set of experts, called journalists, are the ever-present watchdogs, keeping the politicians and their advisers in line. That's a tidy little scenario, but it presents a few problems.

First, and most obviously, it is profoundly disrespectful of people. It ignores what is common to us all—the intellectual capacity to grapple with the human condition and devise creative ways to deepen our understanding of that condition. Experts have no exclusive claim to that capacity; in fact, after two decades of work in journalism and universities, I have concluded that experts are more often a barrier to such creative thinking because they overwhelmingly serve the interests of power, not people.

Second, Oppel's view reinforces a tendency in this culture that is terribly destructive to democracy, the isolation of citizens. We come to understand the world not by sitting home alone pondering, but by engaging in collective action—sharing experiences, hashing through analysis, coming to judgment about how to act, and acting.

That requires organizations. I understand why many people say "I'm not a joiner; I don't like groups." Working in groups often is messy and difficult, but groups are the primary way in which we refine our thinking and act in ways that matter. This is especially true in a society such as ours, in which grotesque inequities in the distribution of power and resources mean that a few people have inordinate access to the political process.

The only effective counter to the unjust control of politics by the wealthy is organization: people coming together to act collectively. Contrary to Oppel's description of public hearings as a refuge for cranks, such hearings are an important vehicle for people involved in organizations to speak to their representatives. Although hearings, like any political process, have their flaws, they are far more trustworthy than decision-making by experts.

Oppel does one other serious disservice to politics by suggesting that most people are working too hard to participate. Indeed, in a society that treats people like profit-generating machines, many of us often find ourselves too tired to do much beyond go to our jobs and attend to our personal lives. However, politics is not a burden but an antidote to that problem. Working with others we not only can change the conditions that seem to trap us but also connect in ways that can recharge, not deplete, our energy and imagination.

Although my own interests lead me to focus more on national and international affairs than city politics, I can attest to the way in which political work—that task of analyzing society and acting to change it, even when the cause one fights for seems lost—is a source of great joy. And it's crucial to keep in mind that when we claim the right to be involved, not only by voting but by asserting our central place in the process through organizing and acting, we are striking a blow not only for a specific issue, but for substantive democracy more generally.

I have no doubt that Oppel offers his conception of democracy in good faith. My disagreement is about where we should put our faith: in the powerful and those who serve them, or in ordinary people. For me, it's an easy call.

Although I have my own criticisms of Austin and its political culture, one of the things I have always appreciated about the place is that many people here still believe in democracy, with all its maddening problems and limitless possibilities. Folks here understand that strong bladders make strong democracies.

Fighting the Good Fight in Texas

Since 1954, the *Texas Observer* has been providing an alternative to the overwhelmingly conservative politics and media of the state. It originated as a journal for progressive Democrats and has stayed that course most of its history. Although the circulation numbers have never been high, the magazine has a solid reputation in Texas, among progressives and journalists.

I started contributing articles and book reviews in the late 1990s, working with Michael King, one of the coeditors then and a great writer himself. I was not constrained by the Democratic Party allegiances of much of the subscriber and contributor base of the magazine; Michael didn't place limits on what I could write. One of the pieces I contributed combined criticism of U.S. foreign policy with an examination of the failures of the news media in covering the government policy.

Covering the naked emperor
Texas Observer, January 15, 1999, pp. 22-23

When the missiles and bombs rained down on Iraq in December, the irony was striking, and painfully obvious: To force Iraq to comply with United Nations Security Council resolutions concerning weapons inspections, the United States and Great Britain violated the UN Charter with an illegal attack. To enforce international law, Clinton and Blair violated international law. I thought the irony too obvious to ignore, even for the normally compliant mainstream press. I was wrong. The issue was, in the words of one reporter I talked to, "the question that can't be raised."

The story is worth pondering, not simply to beat up on the reporters covering (and covering up) this latest U.S. act of aggression, but more importantly to remind us that when we most need an independent and critical press—when the nation goes to war and human life is on the line—we can expect precious little independence or criticism.

The facts are easily summarized: The UN Charter, the foundational document for international law, provides for military action by one member state against another in only two situations. One is when a state is under direct armed attack. In all other situations, nations must first appeal to the Security Council to resolve disputes, and only the Security Council can authorize the use of force.

In December, Iraq was attacking no one. Yet Bill Clinton and Tony Blair did not request authorization for the bombing raids from the Security Council—knowing they would be turned down. So, unless existing Security Council resolutions authorized individual member states to take independent military action, the attack on Iraq was illegal. Did such authorization exist? State Department bureaucrats claimed it did, and when the mainstream press raised the question at all, it mostly dutifully reported that claim without subjecting it to even minimal scrutiny. Such scrutiny would reveal that none of the existing resolutions authorize such an attack.

Michael Ratner, an international law expert with the Center for Constitutional Rights who has litigated a number of war crimes cases, said the United States claim was that Iraqi violations of Security Council Resolution 687 (the April 3, 1991, cease-fire resolution) revived Resolution 678 (the November 29, 1990, resolution that authorized nations to assist Kuwait in expelling Iraq after the invasion). But as Ratner pointed out, "The cease-fire was entered into by the UN, and only the UN can determine if there is a breach."

Francis Boyle, a professor of international law at the University of Illinois College of Law at Champaign who opposed the 1991 Gulf War, said that "at least President Bush went through the motions" and got a Security Council resolution and authority from Congress under the War Powers Act to support that war. Clinton had neither, he said.

"Clinton is standing naked before the world in this aggression, except for a British fig leaf," Boyle said.

In fact, the relevant resolutions appear to confirm that no reasonable case for the Clinton position can be made. (The resolutions are available through the UN Web site at www.un.org/, and
a better-organized list is at www.fas.org/news/un/iraq/sres/) If a
credible, and in fact compelling, legal analysis suggested the
bombing was illegal, why was this the question that could not be
raised? Precisely because the analysis was too compelling. The
answer would have put journalists in the position not just of
saying that the emperor has no clothes, but that the emperor is a
war criminal. And it's hard to get the emperor to answer your
questions at a press conference when you've pointed out his
nakedness.

Still, the question nags: a reporter need not have framed the issue quite so harshly, and every reporter knows how to finesse the
system to inject dissenting views. Why was it so difficult for journalists even to raise the question and use sources who could make
the obvious points? Certainly some journalists, like their fellow
citizens, get caught up in war hysteria, and simply don't care
about distractions such as international law. In other cases, reporters might make the effort, only to find their stories spiked by
more "patriotic" editors.

But from my own experience as a journalist and as an observer
of journalism, I know it can sometimes be more complex. My
interaction with one journalist gives some hints about just how
hard it is to buck the tide when the United States goes to war. I
happened to be traveling the day after the bombing started. I
picked up the local paper and read a story by a staff reporter,
headlined "Q&A: Answers to key questions about the attack."
One of those questions was the legality of the bombing. Instead of
answering it fully the story simply parroted the administration's
standard line: Existing UN resolutions give us the authority to
bomb. No critique of that position was offered.

I happen to know this reporter (we'll call him Joe), and I know
him to be a thoughtful person, both about international affairs and
the limits of mainstream news media. So, I called Joe and suggested his story was incomplete. I offered the names of several
legal experts who could provide the analysis. Joe said that he was
working on a story for the next day about local experts' reactions
to the bombing and that he would keep my points in mind. The

next day's story included some critical views of the bombing, but mostly on pragmatic grounds. The local human-rights lawyer tapped for comment sidestepped the issue, acknowledging that there was no UN authority for the attack, but adding that "'legal' may not be the most important concept here."

So, Joe's first story raised the question but buried it under administration obfuscation. The second story buried it further by giving the administration distortions the blessing of a human-rights lawyer.

A few days later, Joe and I talked in detail about the incident. He said that initially he had felt he had struck a blow for critical journalism simply by including the legal question in the first day's Q&A, since most papers were ignoring the issue completely. My call had caught him off-guard, he said, and made him think twice about his small victory. Joe said he had thought that the way in which he had written the story would telegraph to readers that the administration's rationalization was shaky, but that I was probably right in suggesting that wouldn't happen. Reporters often sneak in "a coded reference to some frightening topic, but don't realize that readers don't know the code," he said.

When I pressed the critique, suggesting that his second story had not been an improvement, he bristled a bit. He fell back on a defense of neutral procedures. He had been given an assignment to get expert reaction. He had called a variety of experts, most of whom he did not know well enough to know their position. They had said what they said, and he put it in the paper. But given that he knew a compelling alternative analysis existed and he knew who could provide it, I responded, had he not failed readers by ignoring it in the story?

Joe countered: His assignment was to get expert reaction, not to get all possible expert reactions or any specific reaction. The more I pressed, the more he leaned on the neutrality argument. Such an argument is common from journalists. What made the interaction with Joe somewhat surreal is that he and I have had a number of discussions over the past decade about the limits of mainstream journalism and the problems with the cult of objectivity and neutrality. We had talked many times about how structural forces limited the political spectrum in the United States. Yet, when pressed, he was relying on a modified and slightly more deft version of the same old arguments.

We split the lunch check and parted on friendly terms. I still consider him one of the more thoughtful reporters I know. Despite our disagreements about particulars of this story, we weren't far apart on our critique of the industry. As Joe put it, "This great machine decides what the questions are, and we scribes implement the script." And on this story, we both knew, the script called for no discussion of simple points that would lead to simple conclusions: that the U.S. attack was illegal, and the U.S. president and top advisers should be hauled into international court and convicted of war crimes.

Bush Protest

Articles and essays can arise not only out of research and analysis, but also out of political actions. Such was the case when George Bush and Brent Scowcroft came to Austin, and our local antiwar group decided to use the opportunity to try to gain some attention for the issue of the economic embargo on Iraq. My attempt to ask a question from the gallery, and subsequent arrest, was mostly ignored by local media, but the fallout from the charge against me turned out to provide several opportunities to raise the issues.

Right after the event, I wrote a long version of the affair that focused on the Iraq issue. It was posted on ZNet, the Z Magazine Web site that has developed into an important clearinghouse of information for left activists (www.zmag.org). But after some time passed and the court proceedings dragged on, I wanted to write more about what the incident said about our degraded political culture.

So, I sent that piece to the Los Angeles Times op/ed page, where it was accepted, copy-edited, and slotted to appear. But the piece never ran. I assume that given the large number of op/eds from which they can choose, the editors simply never rated my piece high enough that it made it to the top of the heap.

The story has a happy ending, however, on two fronts. First, that interaction established a personal connection to an editor at the *Times,* and the paper later published a piece of mine about the Gulf War. More important, the rejection made me rethink the audience for the piece about my arrest, and rather than send it to another mainstream paper I decided to submit it to the *Progressive Populist,* which describes itself as "a newspaper from the Heartland that believes people are more important than corporations." The biweekly paper, which began in 1995, runs articles and commentaries from a range of populists and progressives, and it seemed like a good home for the piece. Editor Jim Cullen agreed, and it appeared in that paper.

As is often the case with an essay these days, the initial publication in print of the piece was not the end of the story. I received some feedback when the piece first appeared, but the email picked up when the essay began to float around the Internet. At one point, I started getting dozens of email messages about it from the Middle East, and later I found out that a columnist in the *Jordan Times,* an independent paper published in Amman, had written about my piece and quoted liberally from it.

Politics in the U.S.: No questions, please
Progressive Populist, May 1, 2000, p. 6

Here in the United States, a democracy with legal guarantees of freedom of speech, I was arrested for asking a question about public policy of a former public official in public. More than a year later, I'm still waiting to find out if I will be punished for that basic act of citizenship.

Here's how it all started: During a break in a book reading by former President George Bush in the Texas House of Representatives chambers in November 1998, I stood up in the gallery and loudly asked a question about his support for the economic sanctions on Iraq that have killed more than 1 million civilians.

It was not an "authorized" question-and-answer period, but there was no stated ban on asking a question at that moment. I had waited until Bush had finished and did not interrupt his speech. I was loud in order to be heard, but I posed no threat and was not carrying anything that could have been misidentified as a weapon. I left without hesitation when a state trooper asked. The only person at risk was me; the woman next to me was so angry that I thought she was going to impale me with her umbrella.

I got out alive, with a serious scolding from the woman for being impolite. I also was charged with a class B misdemeanor for "disrupting a public meeting." A county judge has thrown out the charge on a technicality, and now I'm waiting to find out if the prosecutor will file amended charges and start the process all over. *(Note: Amended charges were not filed by the deadline, which means I won't be charged again.)*

In one sense, there's not much at stake in this case. I'm a tenured professor with lots of status and privilege. If convicted, I would face a fine and some community service. But there are two reasons I didn't want my lawyer to plea bargain.

My first concern has to do with freedom of speech and a meaningful political process.

Certainly, no one individual should expect the right to walk into a meeting and take control of the discussion. But arresting me for simply asking a question that did not disrupt the meeting was clearly a political decision. If I had stood up and told George Bush that I thought he was the greatest president in history, I may well have been asked to sit down and be quiet, but I wouldn't have been arrested. They hauled me out of the room because of the content of my speech, which goes directly against what in First Amendment law is called content-neutrality—the doctrine that the government can't discriminate based on the content of the speech.

My question came during the opening of the annual Texas Book Festival, which is usually fairly apolitical. But that year, the presence of Bush and former national security adviser Brent Scowcroft turned that opening event into a Republican Party party, with the usual political cronies in attendance. It was one more scripted political event so typical of public life in the television age.

Rather than seeing my intervention as a disruption, folks should have been grateful. Along with the other member of our political group who stood up after me and also was arrested, I tried to force some real politics—public discussion of important policy questions—into the event. If we are to recover a sense of politics and democracy that goes beyond TV commercials and pseudo-events, such interactions are crucial.

But my concern is not limited to the state of the political process. I stood up because the ongoing U.S. war against Iraq—a war being carried out through sporadic bombings and the most brutal economic embargo in history—was, and remains, a crime against humanity.

I live in a country that pursues policies which each month, according to UNICEF figures, kill 5,000 children under the age of 5 in Iraq—deaths that are a direct result of the deliberate destruction of the civilian infrastructure during the Gulf War (one of several U.S. war crimes in that attack) and the sanctions still in place almost 10 years later. In the hour that Bush and Scowcroft entertained the crowd and basked in their standing ovations at the Texas Capitol, six more children in Iraq died from the effects of malnutrition, lack of medicine and contaminated water. Although Bush is no longer directing U.S. foreign policy, his appearance was an appropriate place to protest because of his role in creating this crisis.

Why does the Clinton administration refuse to follow the rest of the world, which wants to end the suffering of the Iraqi people and lift the economic embargo? We're told the sanctions must stay in place to force Iraq to comply with weapons inspections, with perhaps the added goal of forcing the Iraqi people to overthrow the Hussein regime. But the sanctions' main mission is simply to break the Iraqi people until we get a compliant government that will follow U.S. orders. The attack on Iraq also serves as a warning to the world: If you defy the United States, this is what happens— we will destroy you, we will kill your children.

In 1996 when interviewed on "60 Minutes," Madeline Albright—then U.S. ambassador to the United Nations and now secretary of state—was asked if the deaths of a half-million children in Iraq were an acceptable price to pay for a policy. She didn't contest the figure. "I think this is a very hard choice," Albright acknowledged. "But the price—we think the price is worth it."

When a high-ranking official believes the deaths of a half-million children are worth it to shore up U.S. power, it is the job of U.S. citizens to stand up and say: "Not in my name will you commit these crimes. Not in my name will more people die."

There is a truism about silence: All it takes for evil to flourish is for good people to remain silent. When we stood up in the Texas Capitol gallery, we were loud. The critical question is not why were we loud, but why are so many so silent?

———————————

Conclusion

Why I Write (for Newspapers)

My clearest memory of the 1991 Persian Gulf War is a few moments on a bus when the world melted in front of me.

I was in graduate school at the time, finishing a doctoral degree and working evenings on a daily newspaper copy desk. I was going to antiwar demonstrations and arguing with people about the war during the day, and then working at night to process the propaganda-like stories that were filling the papers. I felt whiplashed between incredible rage and a deep sadness over what my government was doing and how little I could affect the coverage of it from my desk at the newspaper.

One afternoon coming home from school on a bus, all those emotions broke open. As I sat looking out the window, I couldn't stop thinking about what was happening to people in Iraq, the bombs and the blood; I couldn't shut the death out of my mind. I started to cry. I have no idea if people around me thought it strange; I had no sense of being around people. I felt alone, and I felt a grief as huge as the horror that brought it on. It was a moment when the pain was so raw that I had no defenses.

Nearly 10 years later, as I write this, I can remember looking out that bus window and feeling that despair, and I realize that I have never completely recovered from that moment. There is no shortage of suffering and evil in the world that has moved people, and the Gulf War was in some ways nothing out of the ordinary for a country with a history as brutal as the United States. But it was a turning point for me, a moment after which there was no going back to believing that my country 'tis of thee was a land of sweet anything. It was not a moment of purely rational assessment; it was a moment in which I realized things I had known but until then not completely taken in, a moment of letting myself feel what I had up to then kept at bay.

Later that night, I tried to explain what I was feeling to the one coworker at the newspaper, a man a decade older than I, who I thought could understand. "I know what you mean," he shrugged. "That's what happened to a lot of us during Vietnam. There's no going back. It's never the same again."

That feeling comes back to me often. It came back on a day in May 2000, as the spring semester at the University of Texas was winding down, I sat down in my office one morning to finish end-of-the-semester chores. I lingered a bit with the morning paper, enjoying the slower pace that comes when the students start leaving for break. As I read a story about the controversy over reporter Seymour Hersh's story on war-crime allegations against a Gulf War general (see the piece in the "They've Got It All Wrong" chapter), I started to get angry about the war—angry about the unnecessary death, outraged about abuses of power that officials of my government take as their birthright, and pissed off about the ease with which fellow citizens accept it all as the natural order of things.

But the anger quickly turned to sadness, and I felt myself slipping back to 1991. I put the paper down and began to sob. All the emotion I had felt during the war flooded over me, magnified a decade later by the knowledge of how the crippling effects of the economic embargo on Iraq have made routine the ongoing death and misery. I felt pulled back into that sense of despair.

So I wrote.

I wrote for a lot of different reasons that morning—personal and political, long-term and immediate, strategic and principled. I wrote because I knew the Hersh revelations would be a good hook for an op/ed and that if I jumped on it quickly, I might be able to wedge into a mainstream paper a bluntly critical article. I wrote because I'm expected to write in my job as a journalism professor. I wrote because I like to see my thoughts in print. I wrote because somewhere in Iraq at that moment a parent like me was watching a child like mine die because of U.S. policy. I wrote because I think citizens should know the truth about the crimes their government commits. I wrote because forcing people to rethink the Gulf War often can help in the work to end the sanctions on Iraq. I wrote because writing is a craft in which I have always found pleasure.

But that day, I wrote mostly because I did not know what else to do with my anger and pain. I wrote because when I was done writing, I felt as if there was a purpose for the pain and anger. I wrote because if I hadn't written, I would have felt worse than I did.

I wrote to cope and to vent. And I wrote to be part of a larger movement for progressive change. I wrote for myself, and I wrote for others. I thought about myself, and I thought about the late Salvadoran Archbishop Oscar Romero's plea that those with privilege use it to be a "voice for the voiceless."

But, one might justifiably ask, does one op/ed in one paper really mean anything?

Though it is silly to think that writing in and of itself will bring change, it is not silly to believe in the power of writing. Most people can think of a piece of writing—whether a newspaper op/ed, a great novel, or a brilliant political book—that changed them in some way. On occasion I get letters from people who tell me that an op/ed or an article I wrote made a difference in their lives. All it takes is one of those letters every so often to keep me writing. Virtually every day I read words that someone else has written that make a difference in my life; that keeps me writing, too.

I may be naïve. Others (including many of my professor colleagues) may be right—you can't beat the system, so you might as well cut the best deal you can, find work that is satisfying personally, and be comfortable. "I admire what you do," one colleague told me, "but I have to live in the real world."

The last time I checked, I do live in the real world. It is a world full of injustice and pain and suffering, along with joy and love and solidarity. It is also a world in which we must live with uncertainty, both moral and practical. I can never know with absolute certainty that what I believe will turn out to be right, or that the choices I make to act on those beliefs will be most effective.

After I'm long dead and perhaps someone can assess the political effects, it may turn out that all the words I wrote had no tangible effect on the world, that I was kidding myself by thinking those words would make a difference. Maybe I am wasting my time. But even if I knew all that to be true, I would still write.

I write because I hurt, and because I see others hurting.

I write not because of who I am, but because of who I want to be.

I write because sometimes I don't know what else to do.

I write not because I don't understand what the "real" world is all about, but because I want to believe that we can make real another kind of world.

I write to keep the world from melting in front of me.

Bibliography

In addition to books cited in the text, I have included works important to my political development and handy references for activists.

Associated Press Stylebook and Libel Manual. Reading, Mass.: Perseus Books, 2000.

Ayres, Ed. *God's Last Offer: Negotiating for a Sustainable Future.* New York: Four Walls Eight Windows, 1999.

Bennis, Phyllis. *Calling the Shots: How Washington Dominates Today's UN.* rev. ed. New York: Olive Branch Press, 2000.

Berry, Wendell. *What Are People For?* San Francisco: North Point Press, 1990.

Blum, William. *Killing Hope: U.S. Military and CIA Interventions Since World War II.* Monroe, Maine: Common Courage Press, 1995.

Carey, Alex. *Taking the Risk Out of Democracy.* Urbana: University of Illinois Press, 1997.

Center for Public Integrity. *Citizen Muckraking: How to Investigate and Right Wrongs in Your Community.* Monroe, Maine: Common Courage Media, 2000.

Chomsky, Noam. *Powers & Prospects.* Boston: South End Press, 1996.

Chomsky, Noam. *Necessary Illusions: Thought Control in Democratic Societies.* Boston: South End Press, 1989.

Churchill, Ward. *A Little Matter of Genocide.* San Francisco: City Lights Books, 1997.

DuBois, W.E.B. *The Souls of Black Folks.* New York: Vintage, 1990.

Dworkin, Andrea. *Letters From a War Zone.* New York: Dutton, 1989. Reprint edition, Lawrence Hill & Co, 1993.

Frye, Marilyn. *The Politics of Reality.* Freedom, Calif.: Crossing Press, 1983.

Herman, Edward S. *The Myth of the Liberal Media.* New York: Peter Lang, 2000.

Herman, Edward S., and Noam Chomsky. *Manufacturing Consent.* New York: Pantheon, 1988.

Hoagland, Sarah Lucia. *Lesbian Ethics.* Palo Alto, Calif.: Institute of Lesbian Studies, 1988.

Jackson, Wes. *Becoming Native to This Place.* Washington, D.C.: Counterpoint Press, 1996.

MacKinnon, Catharine A. *Toward a Feminist Theory of the State.* Cambridge, Mass.: Harvard University Press, 1989.

McChesney, Robert W. *Rich Media, Poor Democracy: Communication Ethics in Dubious Times.* New York: New Press, 2000.

Ryan, Charlotte. *Prime Time Activism.* Boston: South End Press, 1991.

Sale, Kirkpatrick. *Rebels Against the Future: The Luddites and Their War on the Industrial Revolution.* Reading, Mass.: Addison-Wesley, 1996.

Salzman, Jason. *Making the News: A Guide for Nonprofits and Activists.* Boulder, Colo.: Westview, 1998.

Tuchman, Gaye. *Making News: A Study in the Construction of Social Reality.* New York: Free Press, 1978.

Zinn, Howard. *A People's History of the United States.* rev. ed. New York: HarperPerennial, 1995.

Zinsser, William. *On Writing Well.* 6th ed. New York: HarperCollins, 1998.

MEDIA AND CULTURE

Sut Jhally & Justin Lewis
General Editors

This series will be publishing works in media and culture, focusing on research embracing a variety of critical perspectives. The series is particularly interested in promoting theoretically informed empirical work using both quantitative and qualitative approaches. Although the focus is on scholarly research, the series aims to speak beyond a narrow, specialist audience.

For additional information about this series or for the submission of manuscripts, please contact:

Dr. Sut Jhally
Dr. Justin Lewis
University of Massachusetts at Amherst
Machmer Hall
Amherst, MA 01003

To order other books in this series, please contact our Customer Service Department at:

800-770-LANG (within the U.S.)
(212) 647-7706 (outside the U.S.)
(212) 647-7707 FAX

or browse online by series at:

WWW.PETERLANGUSA.COM